W9-CZI-782

Audit Implications of EDI

Published by the
American Institute of Certified Public Accountants
in cooperation with the
Canadian Institute of Chartered Accountants

Library of Congress Cataloging-in-Publication Data

Audit implications of EDI.
       p. cm. — (Auditing procedure study)
    ISBN 0–7051–172–6
     1. Electronic data interchange.   2. Electronic data interchange — Auditing.
  I. American Institute of Certified Public Accountants.   II. Series.
  HF5548.33.A937   1996
  657'.45—dc20   95–52405
                                                          CIP

1 2 3 4 5 6 7 8 9 0 AudS 9 9 8 7 6

Contents

Study Group

Members

John R. Adshead, CA
Office of the Auditor General
Ottawa, ON

Serge Beaulieu
Aetna Life & Casualty
Hartford, CT

David A. Haeckel
Arthur Andersen LLP
Houston, TX

Carol A. Langelier, CPA
United States General
 Accounting Office
Washington, DC

Yezde N. Pavri, CA
Deloitte & Touche
Toronto, ON

Douglas Pirie, CA
The Coopers & Lybrand
 Consulting Group
Toronto, ON

Staff

Donald E. Sheehy, CA
CICA
Toronto, ON

Jane M. Mancino, CPA
AICPA
New York, NY

Foreword

The primary objective of this study is to discuss the opportunities and challenges presented to the auditor by electronic data interchange (EDI). It covers a number of issues that will be encountered by auditors through their involvement with EDI. The study was prepared by a study group comprising members of the American Institute of Certified Public Accountants (AICPA) and the Canadian Institute of Chartered Accountants (CICA). The terms of reference for the study group were to discuss —

- The technology and its important uses.
- The business risks and audit risks associated with using the technology.
- The need for the auditor to obtain an understanding of the entity's internal control structure when dealing with EDI (this will be addressed within the context of AICPA Statement on Auditing Standards (SAS) No. 55 and *CICA Handbook* Section 5200).
- The internal controls that are important in EDI systems.
- The effect of the potential loss of the traditional paper audit trail.
- The forms of evidence that are available in a paperless environment to assist the auditor.
- Why a substantive approach to auditing may not be efficient.
- The potential use of computer-assisted audit techniques for auditing in a paperless environment.
- The use of auditor's reports on value-added networks or other service organizations.

Appreciation is expressed to the members of the study group for their efforts in producing this study, and to Peter L. Chiddy, CA, KPMG, Toronto; Mario R. Dell'Aera, CPA, KPMG Peat Marwick LLP, New York; and Jerry E. Jones, CPA, Office of Thrift Supervision, Washington, DC, for their participation in some of the study group discussions. Thanks are also expressed to Jane Mancino, CPA, of the AICPA for her participation in the project and to Donald E. Sheehy, CA, Senior Manager, CICA Research Studies, who, at the direction of the study group, undertook the research and drafting of the study.

Dan M. Guy, PhD, CPA
Vice President, Professional
  Standards and
  Technical Services
American Institute of Certified
  Public Accountants

David J. Moore, CA
Research Studies Director,
Canadian Institute of
  Chartered Accountants

May 1995

Chapter 1

Introduction to Study

This chapter discusses general matters relating to EDI, including the definition of EDI for the purposes of this study, the growth of EDI, and the business and general audit impact of EDI.

INTRODUCTION TO EDI

Electronic data interchange (EDI) represents the application of computer and communications technology to traditional paper-based business processes, supporting innovative changes in those processes. EDI is the electronic exchange of business transactions, in a standard format, from one entity's computer to another entity's computer through an electronic communications network.

There is a special type of EDI called electronic funds transfer (EFT), a money transfer system that banking and financial institutions provide worldwide. This study considers EFT simply as the settlement of an EDI transaction. An example of a typical integrated EDI/EFT system for a purchases/payments system is set out in exhibit 1.1. This study concentrates on the upper portion of the diagram.

GROWTH OF EDI

EDI is not a new technology. The transportation and shipping industries were the primary users of EDI in the 1970s. EDI use has grown significantly in a number of business sectors in the past decade, and especially in the past five years. Appendix A discusses the history of EDI in North America.

Worldwide growth is expected to continue at a rapid pace[1] for the following reasons:

---

1. For example, a survey discussed in *EDI for Managers and Auditors,* 2d ed. (Toronto: CICA, 1993), stated that growth in Canada should continue at 25 to 30 percent a year for the next several years.

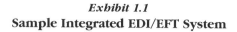

Exhibit 1.1
Sample Integrated EDI/EFT System

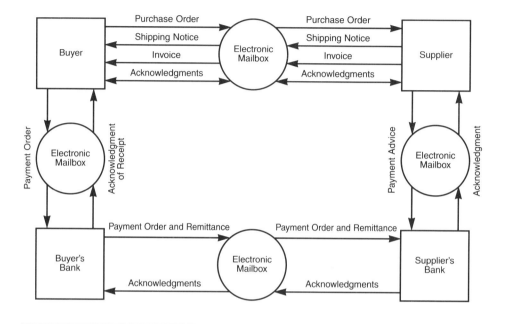

- EDI is a major component of electronic commerce, as it provides benefits that are not matched by electronic mail or fax.
- More entities are becoming aware of the significant benefits that EDI can provide.
- Large corporations continue to push EDI down to new suppliers, creating networks of trading partners.
- Hard-copy documents are being converted into standardized EDI formats, replacing fax or data entry with EDI-based systems.

BUSINESS AND GENERAL AUDIT IMPACT

The use of EDI has created a significant number of changes in the way commerce is conducted and has resulted in the achievement of a significant number of benefits (this is discussed in more detail in chapters 2 and 3). EDI technology is not, by itself, the driver of audit impact. Rather, new business practices that use technology to achieve shorter business cycles, lower the costs of inventory, or meet other business objectives require that the audit team update its understanding of the client's business processes, assess the related risks (some of which may include technology-related risks), and determine how these will affect the audit plan. This is discussed in more detail below.

A client's use of EDI may affect the auditor in varying degrees. Those auditors who are experienced in the use of computer-based auditing techniques and testing computer controls will likely not be challenged by EDI. Those auditors who do not have expertise in this area may find that EDI does represent a significant challenge.

This study addresses a scenario in which EDI is fully integrated into the client's business and application processes (see chapter 2 for further explanation). The extent to which this scenario is applicable to the particular client situation and the auditor's experience with tests of computer-based controls needs to be considered in developing the audit plan.

STANDARDS AND AUDIT CHALLENGES

EDI can be a culture shock for auditors.[2] The change in business practices caused by the use of EDI significantly increases the dependence of organizations on computer-based information systems for essential operations. Paper documents are not likely to be available to auditors to provide evidence of transaction initiation and authorization. To effectively plan and conduct the audit, auditors will therefore need to understand the flow of transactions and may want to gain an understanding of EDI controls. This is extremely important because, in interorganizational systems such as EDI, an employee in one entity may directly initiate a transaction in another entity, crossing both organizational and departmental boundaries.

Generally accepted auditing standards require that a sufficient understanding of the internal control structure be obtained to plan the audit and that, when control risk is assessed below maximum, sufficient audit evidence be obtained through tests of control to support that assessment. They also require that sufficient appropriate audit evidence be obtained to afford a reasonable basis of support for the content of the report.

AICPA	*CICA*
A sufficient understanding of the internal control structure is to be obtained to plan the audit and to determine the nature, timing, and extent of tests to be performed.	*CICA Handbook* Section 5100, "Generally Accepted Auditing Standards," states: "A sufficient understanding of internal control should be obtained to plan the

(continued)

---

2. See *Electronic Data Interchange and Corporate Trade Payments* (Morristown, NJ: Financial Executives Research Foundation, 1988), p. 5.

|

AICPA SAS No. 55, *Consideration of the Internal Control Structure in a Financial Statement Audit*, separately states that "Assessing control risk at below the maximum level involves

• Identifying specific internal control structure policies and procedures relevant to specific assertions that are likely to prevent or detect material misstatements in those assertions.

• Performing tests of controls to evaluate the effectiveness of such policies and procedures."

audit. When control risk is assessed below maximum, sufficient appropriate audit evidence should be obtained through tests of controls to support the assessment."

and

Sufficient competent evidential matter is to be obtained through inspection, observation, inquiries, and confirmations to afford a reasonable basis for an opinion regarding the financial statements under audit.

"Sufficient appropriate audit evidence should be obtained, by such means as inspection, observation, enquiry, confirmation, computation and analysis, to afford a reasonable basis to support the content of the report."

The auditor traditionally obtains some degree of assurance as to the occurrence of transactions from the existence of externally generated paper evidence. Electronic evidence, obtained from the client's computer system, may not provide the same level of assurance as to authenticity and occurrence as does externally generated paper. Therefore, it is likely that audit efficiency would be significantly improved if control risk could be assessed below maximum, because this would allow the auditor to reduce the level of, but not eliminate, substantive testing. As will be discussed in chapter 5, the financial statement assertions that are most affected by EDI are the completeness, accuracy, and authorization of transactions. Chapter 6 provides a discussion of some techniques that could be used.

There are new forms of evidence, such as VAN usage reports, that can increase the efficiency and effectiveness of gathering audit evidence. Also, as discussed later in this study, EDI presents auditors with an excellent opportunity to employ continuous auditing techniques, on-line real time auditing tools and, potentially, new approaches to computerized techniques.

Audit Issues Addressed in This Study

The following issues are the most significant in considering how an EDI system affects the planning and performance of a financial statement audit:

- Knowledge of the business is crucial; this is addressed in chapter 4.
- A substantive-based audit may be less efficient, and a controls-based approach may be the most efficient basis on which to conduct the audit; this is discussed in chapters 4 and 5.
- There is an absence of paper for audit and legal purposes; the impact on the audit is discussed throughout this document and legal issues are discussed briefly in chapter 5.
- Many traditional audit techniques, such as third-party confirmation and vouching, may no longer be possible; this is discussed in chapters 5 and 6.
- Many audit assertions are directly affected; this is addressed throughout the study and, specifically, in chapters 5 and 6.

OTHER PUBLICATIONS

There are a number of publications that deal with EDI, many of which are provided in the bibliography. Various articles also discuss this topic. The business and technology press is a continuing source of references.

Chapter 2

What Is EDI?

This chapter discusses how the EDI process works and provides an example of a typical application.

THE EDI PROCESS

Introduction

EDI transactions are transmitted either directly between the entities and their trading partners or through third parties called VANs (value-added networks) and public networks such as Compuserve, Prodigy, and the Internet. Many EDI networks were established on a proprietary basis among trading partners. The growing use of standards and VANs, however, has established an open architecture through which individual companies can link up with a growing community of users. The receiving entity can receive, validate, accept, and process information, provided it is in a standard format.

Documents in electronic format may be exchanged in other ways (for example, on magnetic tape or disk), and portions of this study may be applicable to such exchanges. They are not, however, included in the definition of EDI as used herein.

EDI-Based Transactions

Although EDI can be appropriate for a wide range of activities, it is commonly used for purchasing, processing accounts payable, invoicing, and financial applications. In these systems, EDI replaces purchase orders, invoices, shipping forms, checks, bills of lading, and other documents with electronic transactions conforming to a standard format.

EDI may change an entity's work flow. Rather than processing a paper document, such as a purchase order, to initiate a transaction, trading partners transmit business transactions through the EDI network.

EDI Transmission Phases

The EDI transmission process normally involves three phases:

- The application interface involves passing the electronic transactions to (or extracting them from) the appropriate business application system (for example, accounts payable or receivable); it is the critical link between the EDI translator and the business's own internal processing.
- The EDI translator involves formatting (or unformatting) the data into an agreed-upon EDI data format and passing them to the data communications interface; all transaction data must pass through this process to be sent from or received by the business using EDI.
- The communications interface involves the transmission and receiving of EDI documents electronically; it represents the media through which all EDI transactions pass.

A schematic example of a typical EDI system for inbound and outbound transactions is set out in exhibit 2.1.

Types of EDI

There are essentially two types of EDI implementation:

- Stand-alone EDI — usually a small pilot project with microcomputer interfaces only. Transactions are often printed, manually reviewed, and rekeyed for entry into the application system. In this situation, there is little change in the work flow and, thus, little audit impact.
- Integrated — application-to-application EDI with integration of the receiver's and sender's computer systems (for example, order processing, fulfillment, and payment).

This study focuses on integrated EDI, although the discussions could be used, within context, in stand-alone applications.

Communications Interface Options

Communication is generally viewed as an extension of the client's existing EDP capabilities; the difference between electronic communications and EDI is not in the technology but, rather, in the fact that —

- Part of the business transaction is initiated outside the client.
- The method of networking may affect/define the business relationships and partnering (see chapter 3).

As discussed below, EDI transactions can be transmitted either directly (point to point) or through a VAN provider or another network.

Exhibit 2.1
Sample EDI System

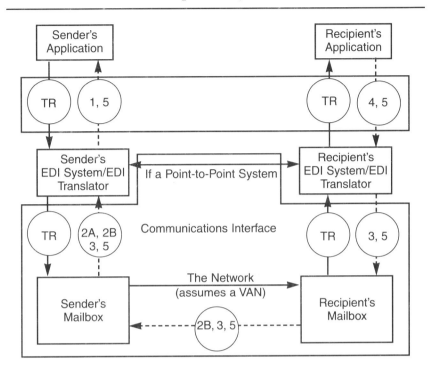

Acknowledgments shown by dashed arrows
Message paths shown by solid arrows

TR: Application-generated transactions,
for example:
(1) Requests for bids, purchase orders,
change orders, payment/advice
OR
(2) Price lists and quotations, shipping
advice or invoices

Acknowledgment Types
1: Status of sender's transactions
2A: Receipt by sender's mailbox
2B: Receipt by recipient's mailbox
3: Functional acknowledgment
4: Status of recipient's transactions
5: Action acknowledgment

Point-to-Point Connection

Under this connection scheme, EDI partners establish a direct computer-to-computer link (a private network). Larger U.S. automakers and governments have traditionally used this method. The advantages for the sponsoring organization include the following:

- The sponsoring organization controls the system; as a result, there is no reliance on third parties for computer processing.
- It allows the organization to control who has access to the network.
- It allows the organization to use/enforce a proprietary software standard in its dealings with all trading partners.

- With the absence of an interim data handler, the timeliness of delivery can be improved.

Disadvantages include the following:

- There is a need to establish the point-to-point connection with each trading partner.
- It defines and restricts business relationships.
- There is a higher initial cost of communication channels.
- There are computer scheduling issues.
- There is a need for common protocols.
- There is a need for hardware and software compatibility.

Value-Added Network (VAN)

This type of network performs "store and forward" functions for the EDI trading partners. The sender transmits data to the VAN; that, in turn, determines the intended recipient for the transaction and places the data in the recipient's mailbox. The data remain in the mailbox until the intended recipient retrieves the document. The VAN provides a cost-beneficial alternative to providing direct EDI connections with trading partners. This type of arrangement has a number of advantages:

- It reduces communication and data protocol problems, since most VANs have the appropriate facilities to deal with different protocols; the fact that the sender and receiver are not directly connected eliminates the need for them to agree on and implement a common protocol.
- The mailbox facility of the VAN allows one trader to deal with many partners without establishing numerous point-to-point connections.
- It reduces scheduling problems, since sender and receiver do not directly communicate; the receiver can, at its convenience, request delivery of the information from the VAN.
- The VAN is more likely than an organization that runs a point-to-point system to provide a third-party report for its customers (pursuant to *CICA Handbook* Section 5900, "Opinions on Control Procedures at a Service Organization," and AICPA SAS No. 70, *Reports on the Processing of Transactions by Service Organizations*).
- In some cases, the VAN provides value-added services, such as translating the application format to a standard format; the partner sending the data does not have to reformat.
- The VAN can provide increased security as it contributes to authentication of sender and recipient and can act as a network "firewall" to protect the entity.

There are also certain disadvantages in using a VAN:

- The VAN charges are in addition to the communication costs.

- The organization becomes dependent upon the VAN's computer systems and controls.
- Because of the involvement of the VAN, there could be a loss of data confidentiality.

These are discussed in more detail in chapter 3.

Proprietary Networks

In some situations, such as health care and banking, industry-specific networks have been developed that allow the transmission of EDI transactions.

Public Networks

The use of public networks such as Compuserve, Prodigy, and the Internet to transmit EDI transactions is an emerging new alternative to VANs and proprietary networks. The use of these networks for EDI exists but is not significant because of an overall lack of effective security for the organization, especially in the case of the Internet.

This study will concentrate on point-to-point and VANs, as these are the most common.

USE OF STANDARDS

A standard is the common language spoken when dealing with trading partners, defining the format of the transaction and the way in which the transaction is communicated. It typically will be a generic, comprehensive protocol, agreed to by a sufficiently wide group of user corporations. Standards enhance development and growth and reduce overall cost. The two significant general standards in place are the American National Standards Institute (ANSI) X12 and the United Nations/EDI for Administration, Commerce and Transport (UN/EDIFACT). At the present time, X12 is primarily used in North America, whereas EDIFACT is used for European and international transactions. This can create logistical problems for entities that use EDI in their worldwide operations. Further problems can be created if the entity is also in an industry that has some industry-specific EDI standards (such as the Uniform Communications Standards [UCS] for the grocery industry).

EDI standards define a transaction set (that is, a data format) for most common business transactions, such as purchase orders, shipping notices, receiving reports, invoices, and acknowledgments. Each transaction set contains defined detail data segments that correspond to the various types of information making up the business transaction, for example, date, name, and address; terms; and the specific details of the quantities, prices, etc. for each of the line items on the traditional paper-based form.

The ANSI X12 and EDIFACT standards are compared/contrasted in appendix B. EDIFACT is expected to become the predominant standard for EDI. No new transaction types under the ANSI X12 standard are expected to be developed after 1997.

TYPICAL EDI SYSTEM

Configuration of a Typical Purchasing System

As discussed in the section "EDI Transmission Phases," the EDI structure is composed of the application, translation, and communication interfaces. If one entity's purchasing application identifies a requirement for another entity's product because a particular inventory level has been reached, or if someone in the first entity's production control initiates scheduled production that requires these items, a transaction with the appropriate information will be passed to the EDI translation software. The process of selecting the appropriate data fields from the various application data bases and passing them to the EDI translation software is called "data mapping."

Building a Transaction Set

An EDI exchange begins with the creation of a transaction set and related detail data segments by one of the trading partners. This usually is done by the programmed selection of relevant data items from application data sets. The transaction is then translated to a standard format. For a purchase order this would involve —

- Identification of those data items needed to build the standard EDI purchase order.
- Data extraction.
- Translation from the environment-specific data format to the standard format required, for example, by ANSI X12.

Building the Envelopes

The EDI translation software will build a transaction header and trailer for the transaction. The transaction header and trailer essentially define the beginning and the end of each transaction and provide summary information that allows for the subsequent computerized checking of the transaction set for accuracy at each stage of translation and transmission. They also contain the parameters that are important to message acknowledgment by the trading partners.

The EDI translation software will also group together all of the purchase orders for a single trading partner and create a functional group header and trailer to form an electronic envelope. In general, the electronic envelope contains one or more individual transactions (in this example, purchase orders) that are combined into functional groups. Each functional group comprises one or more transaction sets of a like nature (for example, purchase orders or receiving information) exchanged between trading partners in a single session.

The software will continue to build a structured train of transactions and identifiers by coupling all of the functional groups for the same vendor and placing interchange control headers and trailers at either end.

Communications

Finally, the communications software uses a header and trailer to conform to the communications transport protocols necessary to transmit the message electronically to the appropriate trading partner.

The communications software is responsible for sending and receiving the long trains of messages and determining if they arrived intact. The application program has as its eventual goal communication with the recipient's application software layer.

Exhibit 2.2 sets out the EDI standard electronic envelope using the ANSI X12 standard.

Exhibit 2.2
EDI Electronic Envelope — ANSI X12 Standard

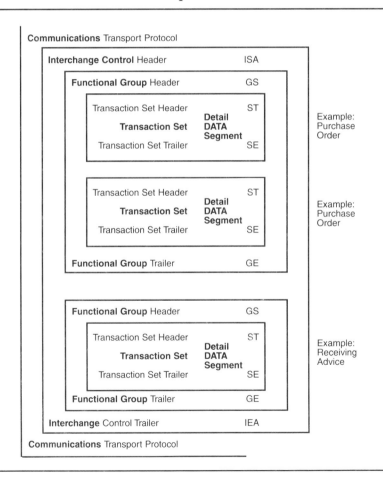

Chapter 3

EDI Benefits and Exposures

This chapter discusses and provides examples of the benefits of introducing an EDI system into an entity. Also discussed are the business exposures that an entity needs to be aware of.

WHAT ARE THE BENEFITS?

The use of EDI has usually produced significant cost savings for the participating entities (see exhibit 3.1 for discussion). As long as the technology is properly implemented with adequate controls, a number of benefits have been attributed to the use of EDI, including —

- Quick response and access to information.
- Cost efficiency.
- Reduced paperwork.
- Accuracy and reduced errors and error-correction costs through elimination of the need to rekey information.
- Better communications and customer service.
- Ability to remain competitive.[1]

These are discussed in the paragraphs that follow.

Quick Response and Access to Information

One of the most obvious benefits of electronic transmission of business data is the reduced time required to process a transaction. This allows the organization to react quickly to customer requests with prompt order processing/fulfillment. Transaction details are sent, received, evaluated, and processed in a fraction of the time usually associated with business processes. This also increases the flow of timely electronic data to management for analysis.

---

1. A comprehensive survey of the benefits is set out in J. Hansen and N. Hill, "Control and Audit of Electronic Data Interchange," *MIS Quarterly* (December 1989), pp. 403-413.

Exhibit 3.1
Examples of Benefits From EDI

The following are examples of some of the benefits that have been obtained from EDI implementation.

(a) U.S. retailer J.C. Penney added more than $1 million to its bottom line in 1991 through savings achieved by using EDI. Through EDI transactions, the retailing giant saved $1 million on processing purchase orders alone and almost $300,000 on invoices.*

(b) Oil companies that have adopted EDI have typically cut administrative time by 50 percent, reduced administration cost by 30 percent, improved customer service by 50 percent, and increased business volume by 20 percent. T. Don Stacy, chairman and president of Amoco Canada Petroleum company, said, "Electronic data interchange has the potential to save our industry millions of dollars, something we desperately need right now."*

(c) Bedford Furniture was approached by Sears Canada in 1987 to implement EDI. One result was the development of "Hottruck," an EDI just-in-time program that allowed same-day deliveries and improved inventory control. In the three-year period following the introduction of Hottruck, Bedford did not miss a single shipping commitment. Without EDI, this program would not have been as successful.*

(d) The automobile industry was one of the early proponents of EDI and helped swell the number of EDI users by making adoption of EDI a criterion for doing business with its thousands of suppliers. General Motors of Canada processes thousands of EDI transactions each day. GM sees many advantages:

- Cost-effectiveness: an EDI transaction costs only 13¢.

- Speed: EDI eliminates five-day mailing time for business documents.

- Reliability: transaction acknowledgments help ensure the delivery of information.

- Flexibility: EDI transactions are not restricted to a paper form – information may be added as required.

- Expandability: additional transactions can be easily added.*

In the United States, General Motors considered paper minimization a strong motivating factor for EDI introduction. Implementation began in its payments system, where the organization was sending $4 billion per month using 400,000 checks to 2,000 suppliers. Complete implementation of EDI was reputed to be capable of saving $200 to $500 in costs per vehicle produced.†

(e) Discount retailer Price Club Canada became one of the more than 4,000 Canadian companies using EDI to reduce inventories, increase profits, cut paper use, and virtually eliminate keying errors. The organization estimates that EDI will eventually save an amount equal to about 1 percent of annual sales, or almost $12 million (in 1991, revenues were $1.17 billion).†

Exhibit 3.1
Examples of Benefits From EDI

(f) The Canadian government is becoming a big user of EDI. Revenue Canada estimates that 80 percent of Canada Customs clients will be using EDI by the year 2000, resulting in the saving of 100 million pieces of paper a year.[‡]

(g) In July 1992, Alcoa implemented an EDI program. The company's decision to design an electronic payments system was driven by its desire to strengthen internal controls in the electronic payment system as well as integrate its payables activities with the efforts of its procurement EDI activity. The company's cost analysis revealed savings of more than $300,000 for a five-year period.[§]

---

[*] *EDI or Die Issues for Canada's Future,* June 1992 (Toronto: Issues for Canada's Future).
[†]Accounting Reformation, Certified Accountant (July 1992), p. 31.
[‡]"The Tools of Survival," *EDI or Die Issues for Canada's Future,* February 1993 (Toronto: Issues for Canada's Future).
[§]National Corporate Cash Management Association, 1993.

Cost Efficiency

While there are some additional costs associated with the implementation of EDI, there are also opportunities for cost efficiencies. The additional costs include the following:

- Hardware costs associated with the installation (Hardware costs vary depending on the type of hardware used—mainframe, mini-computer, or microcomputer.)
- System development costs that vary according to the extent to which EDI is being implemented
- Software costs associated with the installation (The costs of EDI software for a minicomputer or mainframe can be significant, depending on the complexity of the installation.)
- Initial maintenance of an additional data entry system (one for EDI and another for regular transactions)
- Legal and other costs associated with setting up trading partner relationships
- Network communication and security costs
- Training

The business benefits, however, are quite substantial. To achieve maximum benefits under EDI, virtually all data that were exchanged on paper should be passed electronically to a client's application system. This can produce a number of significant benefits, including lower inventory levels (resulting in reduced carrying costs), less waste, improved production scheduling, improved cash management, and more effective purchasing (shorter ordering cycles to help eliminate shortages). EDI eliminates the need for data reentry, reducing overall cost. The levels of cost savings can be quite substantial. Cost savings accrue for every transaction that is undertaken and grow as the business volume increases. It has been estimated that EDI can reduce handling costs between $3 and $93 per transaction. U.S. auto manufacturers have estimated that they save $200 per car in manufacturing costs because of EDI.[2]

EDI also allows for cost savings from economies in data entry. Data that are keyed at the source can be used at all subsequent processing points for a transaction. Rekeying of data by each participating organization is not required.

Reduced Paperwork

The reduction in paper not only facilitates faster transmission of business information, but results in a number of administrative benefits, including, for example —

* Savings from the elimination of forms (mailing costs, form costs, and printing costs).
* Personnel reductions, because less paper handling is needed.
* More efficient filing, storage, and retrieval of data.
* Reduced documentation preparation time.

Accuracy and Reduced Errors and Error-Correction Costs

Data entry errors are normally the most frequently encountered errors in an information system. A properly controlled EDI system can significantly reduce these errors because information such as that found on price quotes, purchase orders, bills of lading, and invoices is passed to and from application systems and does not need to be rekeyed. As a result, errors and error correction costs are reduced.

Errors are also detected more quickly. In some situations, errors may be due not to data entry but to discrepancies in business records (for example, the difference between a quoted price and an invoiced price). EDI facilitates the detection and resolution of errors at the source.

Better Communications and Customer Service

To achieve the paper reduction needed to provide significant cost savings, the relationship between purchaser and supplier will have to be greatly transformed. There is a need for more information on both sides. For example, the purchaser will have to provide information on forecasted future requirements, stock levels, and re-order points; the supplier will

---

2. See *The Role of Management Accounting in Electronic Data Interchange* (Hamilton, ON: Society of Management Accountants of Canada, 1992), pp. 9, 10.

have to be able to communicate information on issues such as agreed pricing, capacities, and lead requirements.

Beneficial new business practices require accurate, timely, standardized-format and controlled data flows between trading partners. Many of these new practices, such as just-in-time (JIT) inventory management, are greatly facilitated with an integrated EDI system. JIT depends on rapid and accurate transmission for ordering and arranging shipping. The time frames associated with preparing, handling, and distributing (via mail or courier) do not support these beneficial business practices. Postage and paper cost reductions are significant benefits associated with EDI.

Remaining Competitive

Two of the overriding characteristics of the modern age are speed and the ever-shorter time in which tasks are expected to be accomplished. Easier, more efficient, and more readily available transportation and communication technologies are allowing data, services, products, and people to move faster. EDI is a technology whose essence is speed.

The use of EDI lends itself to another rising business requirement of the 1990s — customer service. Meeting and exceeding customer expectations is a significant ingredient in maintaining a competitive edge. In general, competitive position is achieved through a combination of service, quality, price, efficiency, accuracy, and timeliness. EDI directly addresses the accuracy, timeliness, and efficiency of data movement.

As mentioned in chapter 1, many different applications of EDI are possible. The maximum benefits of EDI will be achieved when all portions of the business cycle are done electronically and the applications are integrated. Although a number of business risks are inherent in EDI, its benefits far outweigh the risks.

WHAT ARE THE EXPOSURES?

When an EDI-based system is used, a number of exposures are present, including those discussed in the following paragraphs. Exhibit 3.2 illustrates a number of additional potential exposures.

Total Systems Dependence

As an entity's reliance on EDI, and thus its reliance on computer systems, increases, the impact of corrupt applications or undetected errors will be magnified. All EDI transactions entered into by an entity could be corrupted if the EDI-related application became corrupted. If the errors remained undetected, there could be an impact on cash flow, noncompliance with contractual obligations, and adverse publicity and loss of business confidence by customers and suppliers. Undetected errors in transactions received from trading partners could cause losses from inappropriate operating decisions. In addition, as there is more reliance on computer systems and networks, the entity is exposed to disruption of processing and, perhaps, business operations.

Loss of Confidentiality

Sensitive information may be inadvertently or deliberately disclosed on the network or in the mailbox system. Due to the concentration of data, the speed of computer systems processing, increased access to data, and the transaction flow patterns of data, external parties could accumulate and review information about the entity without its knowledge.

Unauthorized Transactions and Fraud

Increased access to computer systems could increase the opportunities to change an entity's computer records and those of its trading partners, enabling significant fraud to be perpetrated. Where payment transactions are automatically generated by the system, payments could be manipulated or diverted, or they could be generated in error or at the wrong time. The benefit of human experience in identifying unusual or inconsistent transactions is reduced with electronic or EDI transactions, which are less subject to visual review.

Concentration of Control

The strength of the internal control structure provided by segregation of duties and structured management reporting may be reduced or weakened in an EDI environment because the number of people is reduced. EDI causes management to place a greater reliance on computer systems and concentrates control in the hands of fewer individuals, potentially increasing risk. While effective automated controls could reduce the potential for human error, the impact of any control deficiencies will be greater and could include overpayment, over/understocking, or over/underproduction.

Integrated EDI trading without appropriate monitoring activity may also result in the processing of transactions in a manner inconsistent with business objectives (for example, ordering from suppliers with which the entity is in dispute).

Reliance on Third Parties

The entity will become more reliant on third parties to ensure security over transactions and continuity of processing. This may create a number of potential risks, including —

- Exposure to weak links or unscrupulous employees.
- Disclosure of confidential information.
- Entry of invalid or unauthorized transactions.
- Incomplete or untimely transmission of data.

Exhibit 3.2
Potential EDI Exposures

Planning & Management	*Interface to Applications*	*Translation*
Improper separation of duties	Invalid transactions	Missing/duplicate transactions
Incompatible standards	Incomplete transactions	Incorrect processes
Errors in internal systems	Missing transactions	Inaccurate processes
Business disruptions	Unauthorized transactions	Untimely transactions
Improper disclosure of information	Untimely transactions	Invalid/unauthorized transactions
Incompatible files	Incompatible files	Incompatible standards
		Business disruptions

Communications	*Third-Party VAN*	*Security*
Unauthorized messages	Lost data	Unauthorized transactions
Alteration of data	Disclosure of confidential data	Alteration of valid transactions
Misdirected messages	Corruption of data	Access to confidential information
Lost/altered/duplicated messages	Invalid/unauthorized data	Unauthorized changes to data
Penetration of systems by viruses	Transmission delays	Unauthorized changes to applications
Network availability/integrity	Inaccurate VAN charges	

Data Processing, Application, and Communications Errors

Errors in computer processing and communications systems may result in the transmission of incorrect trading information or the reporting of inaccurate information to management. If not detected in time, inaccurate or incomplete output may result in inappropriate decisions and potential business losses. Application errors or failures can also result in significant losses to trading partners. This can be more acute if, for example, the EDI application is tied into production and inventory control.

Potential Legal Liability

Where liability is not clearly defined in trading partner agreements, legal liability may arise due to errors outside the client's control. Alternatively, legal liability to trading partners may result from errors made by client employees or from errors within the client's computer system. For example, if an order is received, acted upon, and subsequently determined to be invalid and the trading partner denies sending the order, who bears the cost of having the order filled? There can also be contracted penalties for nonperformance.

Potential Loss of Management and Audit Trails

This is addressed in chapter 5. There will be less paper available for verifying and reconciling transactions. There is also a concern that, without proper controls, data could be lost. Policies for retention of data are also an issue. Normally, EDI transaction data are not maintained for a long period of time. Without proper consideration of legal and audit issues, the entity may not be able to provide adequate or appropriate evidence, in hard copy or on magnetic media, for the legal dispute to be resolved favorably or the audit to be completed cost-effectively.

Reliance on Trading Partner's System

In facilitating just-in-time and quick response systems, EDI creates a dependence on the trading partner's computer system. Errors, security breaches, and processing disruptions in the trading partner's system may have an impact on the client's business operations.

Electronic Evidence and Other Legal Issues

Much effort is being made to define the legal requirements for EDI and to address various questions, such as the following, that are being raised in changing to an electronic system:

- Are the existing legal requirements of writing and signatures satisfied?
- Are electronically transmitted documents legally acceptable and who is responsible if something goes wrong?
- Can electronic data be used in a court of law?

A number of publications are available to the auditor that deal with legal issues and EDI.[3]

In light of the significant impact of EDI, it is important that a comprehensive understanding of the relationship be documented in the trading partner agreement. As an aid, the auditor can refer to model agreements issued by the American Bar Association and the EDI Council of Canada. An outline model of a sample trading partner agreement is shown in exhibit 3.3.

A number of opinions expressed in Canada[4] and the United States[5] provide guidance on situations in which computer-produced records can be admissible as evidence.

---

3. These include B. Wright, JD, *Legal Issues Impacting EDI* (Alexandria, VA: Electronic Data Interchange Association, 1989); B. Wright, JD, *EDI and American Law* (Alexandria, VA: Electronic Data Interchange Association, 1989); chapter 7 of *EDI For Auditors and Managers* (Toronto: CICA, 1993).
4. See, for example, *Managing and Using Microcomputers* (Toronto: CICA, 1991), p. 45, and K.D. Chase, "The Current Legal Environment," *Image Processing* (Coopers & Lybrand Consulting Group, November 1991), pp. 2–4.
5. These include B. Wright, JD, *Legal Issues Impacting EDI* (Alexandria, VA: Electronic Data Interchange Association, 1989), and B. Wright, JD, *EDI and American Law* (Alexandria, VA: Electronic Data Interchange Association, 1989).

Exhibit 3.3
Trading Partner Agreement (TPA) Model

The following represents an outline model of the various clauses expected to be included in a typical TPA agreement. Generally, a TPA would cover these core clauses. It remains a matter of tailoring according to the specific local governing laws and adding whatever other clauses the contracting parties, assisted by legal counsel, would choose to include. This is the case for the American Bar Association (ABA) TPA model, the EDI Council of Canada TPA model, prepared by the Legal and Audit Committee, the Australian model, and various European models.

Outline
1. Identification of EDI standards
2. Identification of third-party service providers
3. Obligation to conduct EDI competently
4. Adoption of signatures
5. Place and time of message receipt
6. Functional acknowledgments
7. Application acknowledgments
8. Garbled transmissions
9. Trade terms and conditions
10. Disclaimer of confidentiality
11. Legal enforceability of transactions
12. Termination of agreement
13. Disclaimer of obligation to enter into transactions
14. Limitation of liability
15. Arbitration

- The American Bar Association Model EDI TPA can be purchased from the ABA by calling (312) 988-5555 and requesting document number: 507-0233-B9. Or simply write to:

American Bar Association
Order Fulfillment Department
750 North Lake Shore Drive
Chicago, IL 60611

- For the Canadian model TPA, you may contact the EDI Council of Canada. The document is called *Electronic Data Interchange Trading Partner Agreement and Commentary*. This document contains explanations of the various clauses with appropriate expert commentaries from the committee. Phone (416) 621-7160, FAX: (416) 620-9175. Or write to:

EDI Council of Canada
5401 Eglinton West, Suite 203
Etobicoke, Ontario
M9C 5K6

Source: *EDI For Managers and Auditors,* 2d ed. (Toronto: CICA), pp. 120, 121.

Chapter 4

Audit Planning Issues

This chapter addresses general and planning issues for auditing an entity that has an integrated EDI system.

GENERAL

This chapter deals with general and planning issues for auditing an entity that uses EDI. Chapter 5 addresses, in general, the controls that may be found in an EDI installation and the related audit implications. Chapter 6 provides a discussion of possible computer-based techniques that could be used when auditing an EDI system.

Audit Benefits

EDI is one of the enabling technologies that change the ways entities do business and, consequently, the way auditors may need to audit in these environments. Consequently, auditors may have to be more innovative in their audit approach.

Some of the audit benefits that should exist in an EDI environment include —

- A compressed business cycle, which reduces year-end account balances for receivables, payables, and inventories.
- Greater thoroughness of transaction data because of the standardized controls built into the technology.
- Improved accuracy of transaction data because of the standardization of data formats and the absence of rekeying.
- Better internal and computer controls because of the consistency of computer processing and, especially in smaller organizations, the formalization of processing procedures and controls.
- Smaller likelihood of material error in financial statement assertions because of the controls in place at the client, VAN, and trading partners, and because of the increased velocity and decreased unit value of transactions that are entered into.

EDI provides the potential for innovative testing techniques, including —

- Computer-based data file analysis and testing of both control and financial statement audit objectives.
- Integrated test facilities.
- Embedded audit modules.
- Concurrent audit tools.
- Electronic confirmation — possible, but limited, application.

These and other techniques are discussed in more depth in chapter 6.

As EDI becomes more widespread, a substantive audit approach may give way to a control risk-oriented methodology with a heavy emphasis on tests of controls, taking advantage of computer-based audit techniques, where cost effective. This is discussed in the sections that follow.

PLANNING ISSUES

Differences Between EDI and Traditional Computerized Environments

The auditor needs to be aware of the differences between an entity that uses EDI and a traditional computerized environment. These include the following:

- The traditional computerized audit environment has boundaries between the audit client and other parties to the transactions. As a result of the boundaries, documents are produced as evidence of the transaction. In an EDI environment, transactions flow seamlessly from one party to another, with little or no physical evidence that the transaction has occurred.
- In an EDI environment, data security and controls need to include the protection of information that has physically left the entity and is en route to other trading partners. The information that is being sent must be protected against alteration, physical mishaps, sabotage, and theft.
- To evaluate EDI evidence that exists only in an electronic form may require the auditor to use data extraction tools that were not essential in a traditional computerized audit environment.
- In an EDI environment, authorization, completeness, and accuracy of transactions may not be as evident as in a more traditional environment. They may be expressed in the trading partner agreement and in program logic, and perhaps evidenced in cryptic digital authentication codes. To assess these application control objectives, the auditor is likely to need knowledge of the agreements and of system processes.
- In an EDI environment, the use of third-party service providers (such as VANs) is prevalent. They present separate audit considerations.

Knowledge of the Business Issues

Obtaining knowledge of the client's business assists the auditor in a number of areas, including —

- Identifying the nature and source of the audit evidence available.
- Identifying areas that may require special consideration.
- Evaluating the sufficiency and appropriateness of the audit evidence obtained.

This is very important when dealing with a client who is involved with EDI. The use of EDI and the resulting impact on client business practices, including those affecting financial reporting, can vary significantly among entities. In many cases, the entity is simply receiving purchase orders in a different form. Clerical control procedures may still operate effectively, and there may be no audit impact. In other cases, however, the implementation of EDI may be part of a major reengineering of business processes.

For example, a manufacturer does not issue purchase orders; rather, it establishes standing contracts with approved suppliers and sends them production schedules and bills of materials. The suppliers ship the prearranged parts and materials to meet the production schedules. They do not invoice the manufacturer, but instead are paid based on shipping and receiving information. The manufacturer regularly audits the performance of suppliers against the agreements.

Another example is the retailer that provides daily sales information from each of its stores to its suppliers, which do business with the retailer under prearranged contracts. They are responsible for maintaining agreed-upon stock levels in each store. Again, no purchase orders or invoices exist on paper or electronically. Payments are made based on shipping advices, and the retailer regularly audits performance.

In each of these examples, the company has changed how it does business in ways that affect the transaction streams that ultimately are reflected in financial statements, and it has changed how it controls purchasing and disbursements. The audit team needs to consider these changes when assessing risk and designing the audit plan. As might be the case with any information technology the client uses, EDI is a necessary enabling technology that the audit team may need to address, but EDI alone is not the determining factor. Any new audit guidance should focus on the need to understand the client's business processes — and *then* the technologies that support them.

When a client has introduced EDI in all or part of its operation, a number of issues will have a bearing on the auditor's consideration of the internal control structure and the nature, timing, and extent of testing. One important complication is that the traditional paper trail diminishes or, in fact, vanishes. This removes one of the auditor's significant sources of audit evidence when testing controls or substantiating a transaction or account balance.

Another pervasive, and potentially more difficult, impact will be the auditor's response to the new forms of business relationships and the profound effect on accounting systems and controls. EDI can concentrate a large number of transactions with a few customers/suppliers. Also, the review of documents, a traditional internal control, disappears. While all automated systems have the ability to run automated controls, it is management's responsibility to design, implement, and test these controls. The auditor needs to keep in mind that the controls are implemented in the application systems that are using EDI and not in the EDI itself.[1]

In essence, the operational and business impact of EDI is that the client will increase the general and application controls (this is discussed in detail in chapter 5). As the structure of the EDI transaction process laid out in exhibit 2.1 illustrates, the transactions are continually subject to implied confirmation and are continually analyzed for correctness. The auditor often may find it efficient to perform tests of these control procedures as a basis for assessing control risk below maximum and thereby reduce the extent of substantive testing.

Audit Risk

The three components of audit risk are —

- Inherent risk — the susceptibility of an account balance or class of transactions to misstatements that could be material, when aggregated with misstatements in other balances or classes, regardless of the existence of internal control.
- Control risk — the risk that misstatements that could occur in an account balance or class of transactions and that could be material, when aggregated with misstatements in other balances or classes, will not be prevented or detected on a timely basis by internal controls.
- Detection risk — the risk that the audit procedures will not detect misstatements that exist in an account balance or class of transactions and that could be material, when aggregated with misstatements in other balances or classes.

Each of the components of audit risk is affected by EDI.

Impact on Inherent and Control Risk

EDI may significantly affect financial statement assertions because of its impact on the nature of the transactions entered into an entity's accounting system, including the initiation of transactions. EDI can affect inherent and control risk as a result of —

- The increased closeness of partnership relations and integration.
- The compression of the business cycle. As a result, the balance sheet may be drastically changed to the point that inventory,

---

1. See "Audit Implications of EDI," *AICPA InfoTech Update* (NY:AICPA, Fall 1992).

accounts receivable, and accounts payable are significantly reduced.
- The increased velocity of smaller transactions being entered into by the entity.

EDI implementation often results in new operational computer systems that produce accounting information as a by-product, for example, just-in-time inventory control systems. In the past, these operational systems were manual or, if they were automated, they were on an independent computer system. Management could reconcile output from operational and accounting systems or compare them for reasonableness. EDI often brings these systems together. The ability for independent reconciliation between trading partners or VANs, company EDI applications, and internal business applications can be embedded in automated routines. This could reduce control risk.

Conversely, management's dependence on computer-based systems may increase control risk. Because of the complexity of integrated EDI systems, it can be more difficult to implement management detective control methods that use external data or evidence.

Consider, for example, companies in the retailing industry that send inventory status and sales information by location to their suppliers. Based on this information and the planned inventory levels predefined by the retailer, the vendor ships the necessary quantities to replenish the retailer's shelves. On receipt of the goods, the retailer pays based either on the electronic shipping notice, usually sent when the vendor's truck leaves the loading dock, or on confirmation from the stores that the goods have been received. These electronic messages, substituting for an invoice, are valued and extended by the retailer, not the vendor. Price, shipping cost, data, and other terms are defined in the trading partner agreements and built into both their computer applications.

In this example, it would be difficult for management to create effective detective controls external to the EDI computer applications. Control over receipt of the goods may have to be accomplished by automatically reconciling actual receipt with "anticipated" receipts generated by the operational systems of the retailer or the vendor. Also, the extinct purchase order and invoice used to be important trigger points for initiating the recording of financial activity and externally designed control points. EDI causes the control points to occur earlier. It should also be noted that EDI does not eliminate the need to validate receipts before payment.

Another result of EDI is that routine reporting periods between trading partners based on an accounting period cycle are eliminated. For example, a monthly vendor statement may not be provided. Reconciliations are more apt to be performed by product line, season, or some other operational factor, thus removing the ability for an externally generated control process based on the end of an accounting cycle, such as a monthly accounts receivable statement. As a result, potential adjustments may not be identified in the same accounting period.

Also, the EDI trading partner agreement could change business practices by creating different payment terms to motivate vendors to provide products to customers within very strict time limits. An example is pay on production, where the purchaser pays for goods only after they are used in production, instead of on receipt. This has an extensive impact on the following business processes for the customer and the vendor:

- It changes the payment terms and, occasionally, the control point for determining when a liability exists. Receiving information may be replaced with production information as the control point for recording a liability.
- The issue of when title has passed should be detailed in the trading partner agreement. This should also address which entity has risk of loss in relation to title passage.
- It causes a loss of the traditional paper audit trail. This occurs because the liability is now being recorded as each individual item is used (rather than when an invoice is received). The customer's accounting system is now completely dependent on the operational system tracking the use of goods already received.
- The vendor also depends on the customer's operational and accounting systems to provide information to record a sale. If these transactions are material to the vendor, the vendor's auditors may need to consider whether the customer's applications are essentially part of the vendor's applications and whether additional audit procedures may be necessary.

All of these can have an impact on inherent and control risk.

Impact on Detection Risk

The potential complexity of EDI systems can increase detection risk (issues that significantly impact detection risk were discussed in the section "Differences Between EDI and Traditional Computerized Environments"). This can be mitigated if the auditor is able to assess control risk at below maximum and thus to accept this higher level of detection risk without allowing it to increase overall audit risk. The auditor may therefore need to become familiar with computer-based controls and computer-based audit techniques. Discussions of possible techniques and controls are set out in chapter 6 and appendix C.

The Use of VANs and Other Third-Party Service Providers

Chapter 2 discussed the use of third-party service providers for EDI. In these situations, the trading partners rely on the third party to route the EDI transactions and, in many cases, to provide translation, storage, and other processing. It is important that the provider have sufficient computer controls and procedures in place to ensure that the transactions are communicated and processed correctly and are not inappropriately disclosed.

Professional standards in Canada require the auditor, when planning the audit of an enterprise that uses a third-party service organization, to determine the nature and extent of the services provided by the service organization to the enterprise and the sufficiency and appropriateness of audit evidence available at the enterprise.[2]

Professional standards in this area are more detailed in the United States. When planning the audit of an enterprise that uses a service organization, the auditor should consider factors such as —

- The significance of the financial statement assertions affected by the policies and procedures of the service organization.
- The inherent risk associated with the assertions affected by the policies and procedures of the service organization.
- The nature of the services provided and whether they are highly standardized and used extensively by many user organizations or unique and used only by a few.
- The extent to which the user organization's internal control structure policies and procedures interact with the policies and procedures of the service organization.
- The user organization's internal control structure policies and procedures that are applied to the transactions affected by the service organization's activities.
- The terms of the contract between the user organization and the service organization.
- The service organization's capabilities.
- The user auditor's prior experience with the service organization.
- The extent of auditable data in the user organization's possession.
- The existence of specific regulatory requirements that may dictate the application of audit procedures beyond those required to comply with generally accepted auditing standards.[3]

When the auditor decides that audit evidence is needed from the third party, evidence will have to be obtained either directly or in the form of a third-party report. When a third-party report is to be used, as is normally the case, its reliability will have to be assessed. The auditor should consider —

- In Canada, the professional qualifications, competence, and integrity of the service auditor.
- In the United States, the service auditor's professional reputation.

These considerations are more fully described in the *CICA Handbook*, Section 5310, "Audit Evidence Considerations When an Enterprise Uses a Service Organization," and in the AICPA's SAS No. 70, *Processing of Transactions by Service Organizations,* as well as in other publications.

---

2. *CICA Handbook* (Toronto: CICA), para. 5310.05. Additional nonauthoritative information is provided in an audit technique study prepared by R.J. Widdowson, CA, *Auditor Reports on Control Procedures at Service Organizations* (Toronto: CICA, 1990).

3. See *Processing of Transactions by Service Organizations,* Statement on Auditing Standards No. 70 (New York: AICPA, April 1992).

The auditor may also consider other available sources that corroborate the evidence obtained from the service auditor. These would include —

- Statements by VAN management describing its responsibilities in maintaining controls and the mechanisms in place to support the control structure.
- Reports issued by internal auditors that address the controls.
- Any other special reports by the external auditors that corroborate the effective functioning of the control procedures.

Use of Public Networks

As mentioned earlier in this study, there is increasing use of public networks, such as Compuserve, Prodigy, and the Internet, to transmit or transport documents and transactions. The auditor should be aware of the following when assessing audit risk:

- Inadvertent disclosure of sensitive information to unauthorized parties
- Computer or transmission disruption
- Hackers and viruses
- Attempted electronic frauds

It is difficult to assess control risk in these networks because they are public and their primary focus is not EDI services.

AUDITOR INVOLVEMENT IN NEW SYSTEMS DEVELOPMENT

Preliminary Review

Because of the significant benefits and changes in relationships that can accompany EDI, the auditor may want to consider involvement in the development of a new EDI system and may want to consider obtaining an understanding of the impact of EDI on the client. The auditor may want to determine whether the proposed EDI system will work as expected and whether the system has appropriate internal controls. This will help the auditor in obtaining knowledge of the client's business and, later, in assessing control risk. Also, when substantive testing is intended, the auditor should ascertain that computer-assisted audit techniques (CAATs) or other procedures can be developed in time and that access to appropriate data is possible. Such involvement would also allow the auditor to have embedded audit modules designed during the development phase (see chapter 6 for a discussion of embedded audit modules).

When reviewing the proposed controls, the auditor should review the general management and application controls to ensure that adequate controls are planned. For example, these might include controls to identify and highlight authorized transactions or duplicate or missing transactions arising from input or application errors, recovery-restart errors, or deliberate disruption. This could be done in coordination with the internal auditors of the organization. An adequate contingency program should also be developed during the system development. As discussed in chapter 5, it is important that controls be preventive rather than detective in nature.

Hard copy, data, and document management procedures and audit trails should be adequate for settling disputes, reconciling transactions, reconciling charges, establishing accountability, and conducting the audit. Frequency of archiving and data retention should be considered.

AUDIT APPROACH

Substantive Approach Versus Tests of Controls

Because of the impact of EDI on the client's business, a substantive audit approach may no longer be cost-effective. It should be noted that effective application and general controls are important for effective EDI transaction processing. As a result, there should be a number of effective internal controls and the auditor should be able to assess control risk at below maximum.

To assess control risk at below maximum, the auditor will need to be able to perform tests of controls. This involves knowledge of the controls that should be present (addressed in general in chapter 5 and in appendix C) and knowledge of the audit techniques that might be followed. Appendix C also sets out a general audit program that might be considered when performing tests of controls and conducting substantive tests in an EDI environment.

Relating Controls to Financial Statement Assertions

For an audit to be effective and efficient, the auditor should ensure that the computer controls are properly related to the appropriate financial statement assertion. This is discussed in depth in chapter 5 following the discussion of EDI specific controls.

EDI Controls and Audit Implications

This chapter addresses, in general, computer controls that should exist in an EDI system and their related audit implications.

INTRODUCTION

Control objectives for EDI systems are essentially the same as those for any information system. The nature of some risks and the potential impact of a control failure, however, may differ. These will affect the types of controls the auditor should expect to find.

For example, because of the velocity of transactions and the reduced opportunity for clerical and supervisory monitoring, most controls will need to be automated. Detective, "after the fact" controls will be less effective, and preventive controls will grow in importance. Appropriate EDI standards and electronic acknowledgments are examples of controls that can prevent unauthorized, incomplete, and inaccurate transactions from being processed.

An additional impact of EDI is the absence of paper documents and, thus, of an important traditional body of audit and legal evidence of commitments and transfers of rights and obligations. Innovative uses of encryption techniques are evolving to fill this void.

This chapter will discuss these and other control mechanisms that support authentication in an EDI environment. It will then briefly discuss some EDI-specific aspects of general information technology controls and application controls, and suggest how EDI application controls support the financial statement assertions. A more extensive list of relevant controls is set out in appendix C.

EDI-SPECIFIC ISSUES

Electronic Signatures and Communications[1]

Lack of Legal Precedent

There will not be a definitive answer as to whether EDI messages are capable of creating legally binding contractual obligations until a challenge or ruling is made in a court of law.

U.S. Perspective

There is some question as to whether or not EDI transactions are enforceable in court as contracts. This relates to the "statute of frauds," which generally requires that some contracts be supported by written and signed evidence to be enforceable. There seems to be a growing belief, however, that a well-drafted trading partner agreement can overcome this hurdle. Also, there is a strong argument in favor of the statute of frauds, as it is now drafted, considering recorded EDI contracts to be enforceable, even if the parties have no formal agreement.

Another issue is when messages should be deemed to have a legal effect. This is important when companies fix a daily deadline after which messages will be either rejected outright or processed at a premium cost.

Under the American Bar Association (ABA) model, messages are not effective until they have reached a certain computer designated by the recipient. The ABA model contemplates the use of functional acknowledgments to confirm all messages. Those drafting the model agreement believed that this was prudent, given the low cost of such acknowledgments. This could be valid for many, but not all, EDI implementations. Some entities will not use functional acknowledgments, but instead rely on other means of ensuring successful communications, such as mutual trading partner obligations in the trading partner agreement, and institute the controls needed to ensure secure conduct of EDI.

Canadian Perspective

In Canada, too, EDI poses a legal challenge. Certain contracts must be made in writing and signed by the parties to the contract. Rules of contract formation, including document delivery, have been developed that determine if a contract exists and when it came into existence. In some jurisdictions, such as Ontario, a contract for the sale of goods worth $40 or more is not enforceable unless a written note or memorandum of the contract has been made. The important issue is whether EDI can be used to create enforceable contracts when such written evidence is required.

The issue of electronic signatures usually presents less of a problem in Canada than in the United States because it is normally not dealt with by

---

1. This section was developed from material contained in pages 95–96 and 108–110 of *EDI for Managers and Auditors*, 2d ed. (Toronto: CICA, 1993). The U.S. perspective was provided by Benjamin Wright, attorney and counselor, Dallas, Texas. The Canadian perspective was provided by George S. Takach, partner, McCarthy Tétrault, Toronto, Ontario.

statute. As a result, contract validity can be determined more flexibly in a court of law.

The section "Nonrepudiation and Authentication Controls" discusses the issue of nonrepudiation. If nonrepudiation control is established, the receiver of a message can prove to a third party that a message was from a particular sender.

Nonrepudiation and Authentication Controls

The term nonrepudiation refers to the use of authentication techniques, message acknowledgments, and effective audit trails to decrease the risk of a party's repudiating an EDI transaction. The stronger the authentication techniques, acknowledgments, and audit trails that are in place, the less likely it is that a transaction will be repudiated. Discussed below are authentication techniques, acknowledgments, and audit trails that can be used to support the objective of nonrepudiation.

In the EDI environment, nonrepudiation can be established at each point in the EDI process where information is exchanged:

- *Nonrepudiation of origin* — This technique allows the sender of a message to provide the receiver with irrevocable proof of the origin of the message. It will protect against any attempt by the sender later on to deny sending the message. This control is provided on a per-message basis using encryption.
- *Nonrepudiation of submission* — This technique allows the sender of a message to obtain irrevocable proof that a message was submitted to the VAN for delivery to the specified receiver. This proof will protect the sender against any attempt by the VAN to claim that the message was not submitted. This control is also provided on a per-message basis using encryption.
- *Nonrepudiation of delivery* — This technique allows the sender of a message to obtain from the receiver irrevocable proof that the message was delivered. This control will protect the sender against any attempt by the receiver to subsequently deny receiving the message. Control of this type is also provided on a per-message basis using encryption.

Sender, Recipient, and Message Authentication and Encryption

Authenticating the sender and/or recipient using encrypted unique codes or an electronic signature provides evidence of authorship/ownership of the EDI transaction. The recipient can verify the sender or the originator (entity or individual) of the EDI transaction. The sender can verify that the intended recipient received the EDI transaction.

Message authentication helps ensure that the EDI transaction set was not modified during transmission. An example of message authentication is the verification of encrypted hash total. Message authentication and encryption as control techniques are discussed below.

Acknowledgments

The use of positive/negative acknowledgments also supports the objective of nonrepudiation. The use of acknowledgments should be defined in the trading partner agreements (TPAs). There are several kinds of acknowledgments, and it is important for the auditor to understand the significance of each as it pertains to nonrepudiation.

Types of acknowledgments include —

- Sender to VANs.
- VANs to sender/recipient.
- Recipient to VANs.
- Recipient to sender.

Acknowledgments can include —

- Time.
- Number of bytes.
- Status of transactions.
- Downloaded to recipient mailbox.
- Acknowledged receipt from recipient.

Audit Trails

To support nonrepudiation, sufficient electronic audit trails need to be maintained. The audit trail supports the determination of whether a questioned transaction was correctly processed or received by an authorized party. Effective audit trails need to include activity logs, including processed and failed transactions, network and sender/recipient acknowledgments, and time sequence of processing.

Message Authentication and Encryption

General

The disappearance of paper and the related traditional paper audit trail, the high volume of transactions, and the elimination of human intervention in transaction processing generally require that proper security and control measures exist, depending on the nature of the transactions and transmission. It is appropriate that the client conduct a risk analysis for the potential contingent losses associated with the messages to be transmitted by the proposed EDI system. Such an analysis should consider whether message contents could be disclosed to unauthorized persons, whether messages could be accepted from dubious sources, or whether messages could be changed during transmission.

When the authenticity of the originator or the integrity of the message must be ensured, the client should consider using a message authentication code (MAC). Alternatively, when message confidentiality is the primary concern, encryption should be considered as a means of control. With either technique, managing the automated or manual key exchange between trading partners is of prime importance.

In early 1989, the ANSI X12 committee developed two technical standards for security:

1. The X12.58 security structures
2. The X12.42 cryptographic service message (CSM) transaction set

ANSI X12.58 defines data formats for security structures consisting of message authentication and encryption. ANSI X12.42 provides rules for the exchange of keying materials in an X12 environment. Where it is important to maintain the integrity and confidentiality of data to be transmitted, these message authentication and encryption standards should be considered in EDI technical systems specifications. ANSI supports the use of authentication and encryption independently or in combination. When both techniques are used, authentication should precede encryption for reasons of expediency.

Message Authentication

A MAC is a cryptographic check-sum value calculated by passing the entire message or authentication elements for the message through a cipher system. The sender attaches the MAC to the message before sending it. The receiver recalculates the MAC upon receipt and compares it with the sent MAC. If the two MACs are not equal, this means that the message has been altered in some way during transmission, and the sender and receiver are alerted of the failure of the MAC code to authenticate the message.

Authentication can also be used to detect attempts to delete, duplicate, or insert messages. This can be accomplished by introducing unique identifiers, sequence numbers, or date/time stamps into each EDI transaction.

Encryption

If authentication is used, messages can still be in plain text form and readable by anyone able to access them. To make messages totally unreadable by unauthorized persons, encryption must be used. Encryption is the conversion of plain text data into cipher text data by using a cryptographic algorithm and key. Data are cryptographically disguised in such a way that only the parties with the key can view them in their native form. Encryption protects the privacy of data passing between a sender and a receiver, irrespective of any communication nodes traversed by the message, as only the sender and the receiver are aware of the cryptographic key. The message source and destination identifiers must exist in plain text form, however, so that each node in the network knows how to route the message.

Although the cryptographic algorithm can vary, the two most common types are DES (Data Encryption Standard) and RSA (Rivest, Shamir and Adleman algorithm). DES uses a system of identical pairs of private keys. The authorizer uses a private key to affix the encrypted authorization to a transaction. This is then authenticated by another person who has the identical private key. This can be cumbersome in large organizations because identical pairs of private keys are required by each authorizer/authenticator. DES is, however, the most commonly used standard.

RSA uses a system of public and private keys. For every private key, a public key is published on a specified database. Authorizations are affixed to transactions using the private key. Anyone having access to the specified database can then authenticate using the public key. It should be noted that it is not possible to determine a person's private key from that person's public key.

Cyptographic security can be applied to different levels of an X12 transaction. For instance, it can be used at the transaction level to encrypt payment orders, at a functional group level to encrypt batches of payment orders and purchases in one envelope, or at both levels at the same time. Transaction set-level security is commonly used, since problems encountered at that level will not cause the entire functional group to be rejected.

Hardware Encryption

Hardware security modules (HSMs) are self-contained, physically secure, special-purpose computers that perform security-related processes and that securely store security parameters and/or other sensitive data. They are also used to install cryptographic keys without disclosure to operators. Encryption performed by tamper-proof, physically secure hardware devices is far more secure than encryption performed by software. Typically, any unauthorized attempt to access an HSM results in its erasing all sensitive security-related data.

INFORMATION TECHNOLOGY (GENERAL) CONTROLS

Security

Proper access controls assist in preventing or detecting deliberate or accidental errors caused by improper use or manipulation of data files or by unauthorized or incorrect use of computer programs or resources. EDI does not really change the nature of the access controls needed, but it increases the importance of having a comprehensive controls system backed by strong policies. For example, uncontrolled access to EDI systems could expose an entity to unintended commitments to its customers and vendors that could not be easily voided.

As in any information systems environment that has an impact on auditing, the auditor may want to test control features that deny unauthorized personnel the ability to authorize or initiate a transaction or to change information already in the system. In a growing number of cases, trading partners have access to each other's systems, for example, to obtain information on stock levels, production schedules, and other data. Access controls for third parties, such as trading partners, will take on increased importance.

For example, to ensure that all transactions are authorized, VANs can validate trading partner IDs and passwords and, in some cases, reject transactions that have not been specifically authorized by sets of trading partners. Validation can also be done by translation software or by the client's access control and application software.

Example 1 – A representative of company ABC accesses the VAN, logging in with company (and perhaps personal) ID and password. (For interactive applications, this may be done once a day or may be a dedicated connection.) The representative then uploads (transmits) transaction strings, each with an envelope (appropriate header and trailer records) that specifies a supplier's network address code and contains customer address (and/or other identifying code) and authenticating password, if needed.

The VAN computer looks at the envelope header and files the transaction string in the mailbox of the addressee. If addressee code is not in the table of VAN subscribers, the VAN will reject the transaction string.

A representative of company XYZ accesses the mailbox, logging in with company (and perhaps personal) ID and password. The representative then downloads the transaction string from the mailbox. For each string, the representative checks the envelope:

- Is address correct (to XYZ's address)?
- Is sender address a valid code in the table of approved partner codes?
- If XYZ requires an authentication password, is the password the correct one for that partner code?

Program Changes

Virtually the same controls apply to program changes as to normal application systems development, with added consideration for emergency or urgent fixes.

Retention, Backup, and Contingency Plans

There should be appropriate retention, backup, and contingency plans in place to minimize the impact of disputes or transaction failure. In addition, if it becomes necessary to recover data, the recovery should be accomplished in an acceptable time period. This can be extremely important to entities with significant technology dependence.

Some of the controls that might be considered include the following:

File retention
- Ensure that EDI transaction files are retained for a sufficient period of time and in an appropriate format to satisfy audit, taxation, and business requirements.
- Ensure that they are retained for enough time to allow for settlement of questions, errors, and disputes relating to EDI transactions.

Backup and forward recovery
- The roles and responsibilities for recovery should be set out between the trading partners.

- Alternative ways to transfer EDI information should be examined.
- Contingency plans should be developed by each trading partner, and the trading partner agreement should specify required testing of the plans.
- Off-site compatible equipment should be used as backup.
- Backup system software and file retention should be used.
- The forward and store, forward function should be automated.
- Manual or system verification should be used to ensure that all transactions have been recovered.

It is important that the auditor be aware of the data retention period to ensure that the audit trail is not completely lost and transactions can be audited, when needed.

VANs

Consideration needs to be given to the controls of network service providers to ascertain that sufficient transaction security and integrity exist. Most vendors provide automated controls in areas of recovery, protection against data loss, and error checking. Depending on the extent of services provided by the VAN, the auditor may want to consider obtaining a third-party report when necessary. If the VAN provides primarily a switch/store forward service, such a report might not be necessary. If the VAN provides significant processing, however, such a report will likely be necessary.

In addition to basic considerations of service level, rights, and obligations, the VAN should provide information on issues such as the following:

- The customer's right to data in case of dispute
- Continuing service in case of disaster
- Availability of transaction logs
- Provisions for confidentiality
- Fallback procedures
- Whether a third-party report will be provided

APPLICATION CONTROLS AND RELATIONSHIP TO FINANCIAL STATEMENT ASSERTIONS

Application controls may differ depending on whether the transactions are inward or outward bound. The auditor may want to obtain an understanding of the entire application and any interrelated applications because, once transactions are in process, there may be limited opportunity for further review and follow-up. Segregation of duties at larger clients (especially for input, transaction generation, and authorization) is an important consideration, especially for outbound transactions.

Because a transaction can quickly affect business functions, there is a need for intervention earlier in the processing cycle to act on potential problems, particularly for inbound transactions. As discussed previously, preventive controls are needed because detective controls may be applied too late. Automated controls are needed to compensate for the reduced human intervention in processing. Some of the control requirements for inbound and outbound transactions that should be considered are set out in appendix C.

Application controls should be present to prevent or detect errors that could cause material misstatements in the financial statement assertions. These controls can be directly related to the financial statement assertions.

Completeness

In a more traditional computer application, classic "batch total" sequentially numbered document and control procedures would typically be designed to meet this control objective. In an EDI environment, however, this control needs to be established by the program when the transaction is initiated or received. In an EDI environment, application controls can be built into any or all of the software application, translation, or communication levels to ensure that all transactions are complete.

Electronic techniques in the communications layer determine that each EDI transaction is transmitted without transmission errors. Most communication protocols include algorithms for predetermining values for bits. These techniques can determine whether any "noise" or loss of signal has altered the data in the transmission and automatically request retransmission. These techniques are very similar to parity checking for information written to or read from a computer's data storage devices (tape or disk). The auditor may want to determine if these types of controls were in effect for the audit period.

At the translation level, there are various examples of controls that try to ensure that all transactions that should be recorded are, in fact, recorded. EDI envelopes can have sequential control numbers that can be tracked by the translation software. Missing, duplicate, or out-of-sequence messages can be identified and investigated by each trading partner. The "back of the envelope" or trailer segment can also include a control counter and hash total of the messages in the envelope (as calculated by the sender). Upon receipt, these control totals can be compared by the receiver to the messages received. Discrepancies can then be investigated.

Another way of ensuring completeness at the translation level is through the use of functional acknowledgments; an EDI message response is sent by the receiver informing the sender that the message was received. It acknowledges the receipt of the envelope and notes that the EDI data segments and transaction set headers and trailers (see chapter 3) are correctly represented. It does not verify receipt of envelope contents. The functional acknowledgment is merely a safeguard that both parties' EDI software will understand the data elements in the transaction and will be able to pass them on to the application software.

Application acknowledgments, similar to functional acknowledgments, may also be used. These are handled by the business application software layer and offer more information, or a greater level of understanding of the message. For example, a functional acknowledgment might, in effect, say, "We received your envelope, it contained one purchase order." The application acknowledgment could add, "And we can supply the quantity of items for the price stated."

Another way of trying to ensure completeness is by aging any unmatched entries in the EDI transaction log files. Those that are not reconciled with matching transaction sets should be investigated after some specified period. This specified period could vary by each transaction, depending on parameters in the initial transaction. For example, an EDI purchase order may contain a specified delivery date. The purchase order acknowledgment and other responses from the trading partner should be received before that date. The purchase order could have more than one date, that is, one date to anticipate the acknowledgment and another for the shipping notice and still another for receipt of the invoice.

The auditor may need a good understanding of how the client tracks EDI transactions through its software layers and what reconciliation procedures are performed by the application software, or perhaps by special control programs that analyze the EDI transaction log files and other control files.

Existence/Occurrence

Message authentication, as discussed in the section "Message Authentication and Ecryption," is a procedure that allows each party to verify that data received are genuine and have not been altered. It can be used to detect situations in which there are discrepancies (accidental or deliberate) between the sender's and the receiver's translation software. It would not, however, assist in detecting whether an error had occurred in the sender's application system.

Again, EDI transaction log files could be used to help provide assurance that transactions were recorded in the appropriate accounting period and that the accounts reflect existing assets and liabilities at the audit date. Before the specifics are discussed, the different levels of acknowledgment between the trading partners need to be reviewed.

The functional acknowledgment offers the sender only limited assurance that the transaction sent to the receiver (supplier) was understood per the agreed-upon standards. A separate EDI transaction, acknowledging acceptance of the contents of the purchase order and any implied commitments, is required before the sender can be satisfied that its needs can be met by the supplier.

Valuation

Pricing information for a transaction may come from the EDI purchase order or a mutually controlled pricing catalogue maintained by the trading partners. The review and authorization for processing changes to these periodic price catalogues should also be controlled by the supplier's access and authorization software, and these may need to be addressed by the auditor.

In many cases, the purchaser's trading partners may send priced and extended electronic invoices that can be logged into the EDI transaction log files and recorded in the general ledger by the application software layer. As long as a comparison with the purchase order price is performed, the controls ensuring completeness could assist in determining proper valuation. Access controls over the price file used when the purchase order was created would have to be present.

Depending on the nature of the transaction, standards could be used to check the accuracy of any key valuation fields. For example, a control total of invoice amounts could be included in the envelope and used by the partners to check pricing/cost valuation accuracy.

As the relationship between trading partners evolves, one trend is to remove redundant documents, such as the electronic invoice. When this occurs, the shipping notice or the receiving information provides the valuation. In this case, the auditor may wish to test the access controls and authorization to change prices associated with the trading partners' products to determine whether the accounts are properly valued.

Measurement/Ownership (Rights and Obligations)

A liability does not exist until the goods are shipped or received, depending on the trading partner agreement and the shipping terms expressed in the purchase order. The EDI transaction log file may indicate that a liability should be recorded when the file is updated with information entered from the entity's receiving department; or the liability might arise when the entity receives an electronic shipping notice from the supplier or an electronic manifest from a freight company (that is, Free on Board, or FOB, shipping point). Therefore, the portfolio of EDI transaction sets required to record a liability and the timing of the liability may vary, depending on the terms in the EDI transactions.

The auditor may have to determine the different shipping terms used and, if the procedures contained in the applications provide for appropriate correlation of dates, to enable recording of transactions on a timely basis. Review of the aging of incomplete files or, perhaps, reconciliations of complete transaction files and bills of lading could provide some assurance of the timely recording of transactions.

The use of acknowledgments, discussed previously, can also assist in ensuring that transactions are recorded on a timely basis. A client application or translation system could, for example, identify EDI transmissions that remain unmatched for more than a particular amount of time. One final control would be to use date-and time-stamping for EDI transactions. The VAN and/or trading partners could then investigate unread messages.

Presentation

Controls to ensure proper classification are similar to those in other advanced automated systems. Normally, the auditor would expect to find cross-reference tables using an identifier, such as a part number or customer/supplier number, that assigns appropriate classifications for posting and/or reporting purposes. Details on the initial electronic purchase order could also help in determining the proper classification.

Chapter 6

Examples of Computer-Assisted Audit Techniques

This chapter provides examples of computer-assisted audit techniques that can be used for gathering evidence on a substantive or test-of-control basis.

INTRODUCTION

As mentioned previously, EDI is one of the enabling technologies that change the way organizations do business and the way that auditors may need to audit these environments. In an integrated EDI environment, paper is replaced by streams of electronic data that can be most easily analyzed in automated fashion. Also, the use of programmed controls, rather than manual controls, is likely to increase, and so will the need for advanced automated audit techniques to deal with this environment. The auditor's challenge is how to effectively audit in this paperless, programmed control-intensive environment.

In the course of gathering audit evidence, the auditor should consider the use of computer-assisted audit techniques (CAATs). As discussed in chapter 4, the auditor may need to be familiar with computer-based audit techniques in order to obtain audit evidence of an EDI transaction. The purpose of this chapter is to discuss some of the testing methods available for use in an integrated EDI system. These techniques include, for example, the use of audit software, integrated test facilities, embedded audit modules, and concurrent audit tools. It addresses the possibilities and limitations of some potential methods of testing. It does not, however, address all of the procedures that could be used in a traditional computer system.

In addition, because of the dependency of the entity on computer processing and the fact that the traditional paper-based audit trail disappears, the auditor may want to perform tests of programmed control procedures and is thus more likely to use computer-assisted audit techniques. Examples of procedures are also set out in this chapter.

COMPUTER-ASSISTED AUDIT TECHNIQUES

Integrated Test Facility

Introduction

An integrated test facility (ITF) is a fictitious entity, such as an imaginary company, established on a live data file. It enables the auditor to enter test transactions into the system without corrupting the integrity of real operational or financial data.

An ITF is best used in —

- Testing transactions of automated applications.
- Testing integrated processing where entered or generated data automatically update data files used in several applications.
- Testing when the audit trail is complex and the system makes it difficult to trace transaction flow.

Audit Advantages

There are a number of audit advantages to using an ITF in an integrated EDI operation:

- It is well suited to testing where a paper audit trail no longer exists.
- It is very suitable to on-line systems.
- It allows for more comprehensive system testing, because transactions are entered into the system in a manner similar to live transactions.
- It permits recurring audit checks to be performed with minimal operational difficulty.
- Most, if not all, EDI software vendors provide built-in ITF capability.

It is possible for an auditor to launch test transactions through direct access or a VAN and simulate a trading partner's transaction. The purpose would be to test controls (for example, trading partner IDs and passwords, sequential numbering and reconciliation of transmission edits, message authentication codes) that are part of the organizational systems. If the entity uses a VAN, the test transactions could be sent to the VAN and addressed to the entity. The entity would then authorize the VAN to accept transactions from the auditor and forward them to the entity's mailbox. The auditor could launch these test transactions on a continuous or periodic basis and compare the expected processing results with the actual results.

Another alternative would be to set up audit transaction types that duplicate current transactions and process these back to the auditor. The auditor would need to register these with the VAN. It is also possible to set up a more advanced integrated testing facility where the auditors of both trading partners cooperate in their audits. The integrated facility is set up with appropriate backout of live audit transactions as they are processed through the trading partners' systems.

Example 1 discusses a comprehensive test that verifies the actions taken by the VAN when the transmission is received, the translation process, and, most important, the actions taken by the application. This technique would provide assurance for the functioning of controls, which could be programmed and/or user-dependent. Because the auditor controls which test transactions are used and when, flexibility in the timing of procedures and the quality of the audit evidence obtained are high.

Example 1 – One example of an integrated test facility application is in a large health insurance organization that electronically receives and pays claims from hospitals. Using the auditor account at the VAN, or other access into the organization's system, the auditor submits a series of claims (e.g., dental claims, surgical claims, etc.) via EDI and reviews the claims register to determine which claims were paid and the amount of payment. The test claims include a variety of conditions, including claims both for individuals who are entitled to benefits and fictitious individuals. In addition, procedures such as heart surgery that are payable by the insurance company, and procedures such as cosmetic surgery that are not covered by insurance, as well as charges within and in excess of reimbursable limits, are tested. The test data go through the system and output is routed to the test division or dummy account. This file is then reviewed online by the auditor.[1]

Audit Disadvantages

If a client's systems were designed without ITF capabilities, it is unlikely that the entity will redesign them to accommodate the auditors. Still, management may have no other acceptable alternative. There are a number of implementation considerations:

- Test data must be developed or obtained; it can be a significant effort to design and build a test deck and generator that have the flexibility to deal with various EDI standards that are in place.
- As with any system development effort, the cost of adding ITF facilities can be significant if they were not added during the development phase.
- The required level of knowledge to work with an EDI translator can be quite high, depending on the number of transaction sets and standards used.
- Care should be taken by the auditor to ensure either that the test transactions are prevented from entering the live data environment or that they are eliminated after their entry.

---

1. See C. Zoladz, "Auditing in an Integrated EDI Environment," *IS Audit & Control Journal*, Vol. II, 1994 (Rolling Meadows, IL: Information Systems and Control Systems, 1994), p. 38.

- There is a potential for unauthorized application modifications that identify audit transactions and process them differently from other (real) transactions.

Data Extraction and Analysis (Audit) Software

Introduction

Traditional audit software can be used at both the sender and receiver ends to audit and sample the transaction streams from application logs created within the application's program suite or from the EDI interface. Also, audit software can be used to extract information from the relevant data bases, VAN audit trails, or archive files. Some of the advanced EDI workstations from network providers provide audit trails of work carried out by users at each workstation. Audit software could be written to extract audit information if the precoded audit information retrieval is not sufficient. The auditor can also request audit reports from the network provider in various sequences by inputting EDI audit transactions that reference the audit trail file. These references can then be captured on-line and analyzed by audit software (for example, select transmissions sent between September 1 and September 30, 19XX, in document receiver sequence). The auditor can then use the audit software to sample a document type for follow-up or produce a report to analyze a particular receiver.

With the VAN's permission, audit software could also be used to access the archive file and extract audit information on selected transactions. The auditor would need to check with the VAN provider to find out how long the files are held on-line. Access to earlier transaction information may be impossible if the files are not retained, or difficult if the files are stored off-line or off-site.

Audit Advantages

Audit software is useful when there is no manual audit trail. For example, it can be used to identify outstanding advance shipping notices that remain unmatched with shipping invoices. If the client does not have a similar reporting mechanism, this test could help identify unrecorded liabilities. Finally, it can be helpful in testing the functioning and effectiveness of the control itself.

As EDI evolves, it will provide excellent opportunities for this type of software, since there are standard transaction documents that will allow for portability from one client to another.

Audit Disadvantages

There are various disadvantages to using data extraction and analysis software. In an EDI environment, the lack of data availability may be the most prevalent.[2]

---

2. A detailed discussion of the benefits and challenges presented by CAATs is provided in *Application of Computer Assisted Audit Techniques Using Microcomputers* (Toronto: CICA, 1994).

Embedded Audit Modules

Introduction

Embedded audit modules are programs written and compiled within an application to perform audit procedures concurrent with the operation of the application. These modules may run routinely or function only when specifically activated.

Embedded audit modules enable continuous monitoring and analysis of transaction processing. They are particularly effective in high-volume, on-line, real-time systems, in which the timeliness, completeness, accuracy, and validity of transactions are essential. Such systems do not lend themselves to manual auditing. In many situations, embedded audit modules are implemented for the applications that pose the highest risk for the organization.

It is possible to embed these modules in the EDI system at different levels. At the trading partner entry level, for example, it would be possible to embed a module at an individual EDI workstation level. It would also be possible to embed a module at the communication software level, if all messages went along a leased line. These messages could then be written to an audit file for later examination.

Audit Advantages

The use of embedded audit modules offers a number of audit advantages:

- They enable the auditor to continuously monitor systems.
- They allow the auditor to have specific data samples selected at any time because the data are selected simultaneously with the normal production process.
- They encourage auditor involvement during the system design phase.

Compelling reasons for the use of embedded audit modules in an integrated EDI environment are the loss of a visible audit trail and the fact that transaction files may not be available for subsequent analysis. In many cases, the embedded audit module can be extended with exception reporting and file interrogation facilities. This will provide the auditor with an effective way to detect unauthorized system modifications.

These modules are complex, advanced audit tools. The auditor can use them to select items for review or evaluation (for example, deviations from predetermined purchase and sales policies and frequency of certain types of transactions).

Embedded audit modules are useful in monitoring the performance of the EDI software and the translating system and/or application system on a continuous or selective basis. Even though most systems are designed to prevent and detect errors, errors can occur because of defects in the system's development or incorrect or improper system modifications. Embedded audit modules provide the auditor with an independent check on the performance of the application system and provide an opportunity for timely corrective action.

Audit Disadvantages

Currently, embedded audit modules are not widely used, for the following reasons:

- The time, effort, and resources required to build and maintain them can be substantial.
- They must be protected against unauthorized modifications.
- They normally must be built during the development of a new system; failure to do so will significantly increase their costs at a later date.
- Because of the interrelationships between the module and the application, modification of the application typically requires modifying the audit module.
- They require a high level of data processing/programming skills; use of EDI standards, EDI software, and database structures requires specific technical knowledge.

The reengineering of business processes and systems that occurs during the EDI implementation may provide the auditor with the opportunity to include embedded audit modules in these reengineered systems. Consequently, their use should increase in the future.

Concurrent Audit Tool

Introduction

In general, a concurrent audit tool is similar to an embedded audit module in that it inspects the transaction as it takes place. The main difference is that it is designed and controlled by the auditor and linked into the organization's information system rather than being part of the system.

Audit Advantages

A concurrent audit tool allows an auditor to test the client's controls while a transaction is being processed without disrupting the client's normal operations. The concurrent audit tool can be linked into the system for a period of time to perform tests and provide audit evidence for the auditor.

In a situation where the client has weak controls, a concurrent audit tool gives the auditor the opportunity to perform analytical procedures and substantive testing, because the data has been captured by the tool. When the client controls are strong, the auditor can also use the tool for the testing of controls.

One of the advantages of this tool, in contrast to the ITF and embedded audit module, is the fact that it is designed and controlled by the auditor. As a result, the potential for unauthorized modification is reduced.

The use of a concurrent audit tool is illustrated in the following example.

Example 2 – An example of using a concurrent audit tool would be to test invoices in the client's purchasing process. All invoice messages are intercepted and copied by the auditor's computer (pre-translation) before being passed back to the organization's system for processing. The auditor could select a random sample on invoice numbers and choose all invoices/messages over a predetermined amount. The concurrent audit tool then verifies the previously received shipment as well as the receipt record and the amount payable (if reflected by the client). If the client does not show the payable, further investigation by the auditor is required. Such an investigation could include reviewing the suspense files.

The total number of intercepted messages (in this case, invoices) is counted and compared with the total updates in the client's related database (in this case, accounts payable) for the period the auditor tested. Discrepancies between the amount the auditor expects to be reflected in the client's records and the amount actually recorded provides evidence about how well the system operates and the accuracy and completeness of the balance. These analytical procedures or relationship checks will provide persuasive evidence, because the auditor has evidence of the messages received and has followed them through the entire application/database.[3]

Audit Disadvantages

In general, the disadvantages are similar to those of embedded audit modules.

Confirmations

Confirmations may also be performed electronically between the auditor and the client's trading partners. To work successfully, however, trading-related applications may need to be modified to automatically retrieve the requested information, format it in an EDI transaction set, and transmit it to the requesting auditor. The development of EDI confirmation transactions depends, to a large extent, on the relevance of confirmations in future audits. In an integrated EDI environment, where the higher velocity of transactions could result in immaterial receivable and payable balances, confirmations may be unnecessary. Subsequent payment review would probably be more efficient.

CONCLUSIONS

As mentioned throughout this study, EDI will likely have a significant impact on how organizations conduct their business and is not a technical replacement for a paper-based system. EDI will, for example —

---

3. Ibid., p. 39.

- Change the business relationship between purchaser and supplier.
- Facilitate purchasing strategies, such as JIT inventory purchasing.
- Increase the reliance of management on increasingly sophisticated and complex computer systems, thereby increasing the need for strong controls over the computer systems on which management depends.

There are also a number of standards that organizations need to be aware of in implementing EDI, including —

- Data retention standards.
- Evidence standards.
- Legal agreement standards.
- Data structure standards.

The impact of EDI on an auditor can also be significant, especially if the auditor has traditionally used a paper-based substantive approach. There are, however, no boilerplate instructions that can be given for auditing an integrated EDI system. Rather, the auditor needs to apply professional judgment to each client organization. Therefore, this study provides practical guidance for the auditor in developing a strategy to audit in such an environment.

Brief History of EDI[1]

This appendix provides a brief history of EDI development in North America.

Year	Event
1968	The San Francisco and Los Angeles Clearing Houses convene a committee to study the exchange of paperless entries among banks as a way to cope with growing check volume. Ten California banks form the Special Committee on Paperless Entries (SCOPE) to recommend specific procedures for paperless payments and deposits through such methods as the exchange of magnetic tapes. Transportation industry forms the Transportation Data Co-ordinating Committee (TDCC), having recognized the problem of communicating with different formats, protocols, and line speeds. TDCC begins to design the basic logic for a system of electronic messages for the transportation industry.
early 1970s	National Data Corporation and others establish computer service bureaus.
1970	American Bankers Association forms the Monetary and Payments System Committee to address the needs of the payments system. It recommends industry standards and a comprehensive nationwide settlement system of paperless entries.
1971	Several Atlanta banks form a Committee on Paperless Entries (COPE).

1. Much of this data has been taken from *Electronic Data Interchange and Corporate Trade Payments* (Morristown, NJ: Financial Executives Research Foundation, 1988), pp. 7–10, and "The History of Canadian EDI," EDI Forum, Vol. 6, No. 1 (Oak Park, IL: EDI Group, Ltd.), pp. 73–77.

Year	Event
1972	The San Francisco Federal Reserve Bank and its Los Angeles branch start to operate the first automated clearinghouse.
1973	National Automated Clearing House Association (NACHA) is formed under the auspices of the American Bankers Association to develop a framework in which regional clearing house associations can exchange information on behalf of their member banks.
mid 1970s	National Data Corporation, General Electric, and others develop systems within their time-sharing networks for banks to store and for customers to retrieve balance and transaction information.
1975	Automated Clearing House (ACH) network begins to process Social Security payments. Other nationwide applications follow, such as veterans' payments and military payrolls. Insurance companies begin to debit premiums and pay claims to individuals through the ACH. TDCC (now the Electronic Data Interchange Association [EDIA]) publishes U.S. EDI standards.
1976	American Hospital Supply Corporation (now part of Baxter Healthcare Corporation) introduces ASAP, a proprietary computer order-entry system. Large retailers such as Sears, J. C. Penney, and K Mart develop proprietary standards for ordering from their suppliers.
1978	Federal Reserve implements interregional exchange among automated clearinghouses. Six major trade associations in the grocery industry commission Arthur D. Little, Inc., to study the feasibility of electronic data interchange among food manufacturers, distributors, and brokers. The study analyzes how electronic communications could make basic ordering and invoicing functions more efficient. It recommends the use of a store-and-retrieve system for communications and grocery industry adaptation of the TDCC message format system.
1978/ 1979	American National Standards Institute (ANSI) forms Accredited Standards Committee (ASC) X12 to develop uniform, variable-length, cross-industry standards. It builds on the message format system developed by the TDCC. Federal Reserve begins processing debits through the night processing cycle, allowing companies to make deposits in outlying

Year	Event
	locations late in the day, provide their banks with instructions to move funds through the ACH, and have use of those funds in their central concentration accounts the next morning. NACHA Board of Directors appoints a task force to study corporate trade payments.
1980	Uniform Communications Standards Committee (UCSC) is formed by the grocery industry associations that commissioned the Arthur D. Little study. The committee embarks on a six-month project to develop EDI transaction set formats based on the TDCC architecture.
1981	The Automobile Industry Action group, a not-for-profit trade association, is formed by members of middle management in vehicle manufacturing companies and their suppliers. NACHA introduces the first corporate trade payment formats, Cash Concentration or Disbursement (CCD) and the Corporate Trade Payment (CTP). Banks begin to sell corporate trade payments though the ACH network as an alternative to paper checks.
1982	Joint Electronic Data Interchange (JEDI) is formed to combine dictionaries. EDI pilots are developed in Canada under the auspices of the Grocery Products Manufacturers of Canada (GPMC) and another by the drug industry.
1983	ANSI X12 publishes first standards; ANSI X12 standards become umbrella standards for cross-country standards. Canadian grocery industry adopts modified version of UCS message standard (to allow metric trade).
1984	Chemical industry commissions CIDX, an industry association for the implementation of EDI. It adopts the ANSI X12 standards and concentrates most of its efforts on implementation.
1984	EDIFACT West European Technical Assessment Group produces an EDI standard that later became the basis for EDIFACT.
1985	EDI Council of Canada formed.
1986	General Motors announces a program to pay its suppliers electronically.

Year	Event
1987	U.S. Treasury Department starts a program to replace an annual volume of 80 million vendor check payments with ACH payments. NACHA implements Corporate Trade Exchange (CTX) format as a cooperative effort with ASC X12. ASC X12 and Grocery Industry Uniform Code Council (UCC) discuss possible merger. Warehousing Industry Network System (WINS) and UCC propose merging standards. ISO 9737 (international syntax) approved.
1988	First EDIFACT standard is voted on; strong support exists for United Nations-backed EDI for Administration, Commerce and Transport standard.
1989	Canadian Inter-Financial Institutions EDI Committee formed, responsible for establishing standards for financial institutions exchanging transactions with each other through EDI.
1992	Canadian Payments Association approves Standards and Guidelines Applicable to EDI Transactions (CPA Standard 023). These govern the exchange of EDI transactions between Canadian financial institutions that are members of the Canadian clearing system.

Brief Comparison of EDI Standards

This appendix discusses the difference between the two significant EDI standards in use today. It should be noted that EDIFACT is the emerging standard for transacting business worldwide.

GROWTH OF TWO STANDARDS

Why Standards?

In an advanced economy, standards for EDI are essential to enhance growth and use and to reduce costs. EDI originally developed along specific-industry lines, with each industry developing its own standards. As the use of EDI grew, so did the need for cross-industry common standards. The alternative would be for each industry to support at least three standards — the standard for its own industry, the X12 North American standard, and the EDIFACT European standard.

In the United States, the American National Standards Institute (ANSI) created the Accredited Standards Committee (ASC) X12. Its goal was to establish EDI standards that would cross all industry segments. Various subcommittees were formed to develop standards that would accommodate and consolidate industry standards; their overall goal was to emerge with one common, generic, public standard. X12 became the pervasive standard in North America.

Because international commerce requires fast, efficient, and accurate information, ideally there should be a single set of EDI standards covering all EDI message types. EDIFACT (United Nations/EDI for Administration, Commerce and Transport) has been developed as a specific solution to these universal requirements (also addressed by ANSI). This standard, promoted by the UN, has been adopted in many parts of the world and is expected to eventually become the predominant standard.

The integration of international trade (NAFTA, the European Union, etc.) will further necessitate the use of one common standard worldwide. As it now stands, X12 is mature and relatively more stable than EDIFACT. EDI-

FACT, however, is catching up. Ultimately, it is anticipated that X12 will migrate to or merge with EDIFACT. A survey of industry membership has determined that some 70 percent are in favor of one common standard for worldwide trade. The ultimate objective would be to establish EDIFACT as the common standard.

STANDARDS COMPARISON

X12

The EDI electronic envelope at the interchange level is a package containing one or more documents, such as purchase orders and invoice payments, grouped into functional applications. It was discussed in chapter 2 and is composed of —

- Headers and trailers to provide basic control structure.
- A functional group (one or more transaction sets of a similar nature).
- A transaction set (one complete electronic document).

The ANSI X12 Standard Code for Headers and Trailers as shown in the envelope are as follows:

- ISA — Header Start Interchange
- IEA — Trailer End Interchange
- GS — Header Start Functional Group
- GE — Trailer End Functional Group
- ST — Header Start Detail Segment (Message)
- SE — Trailer End Detail Segment

The control codes trigger the beginning or the end of an item, so there is a predetermined and controlled flow of data items.

EDIFACT

The EDIFACT standard provides control features in the headers and trailers of its interchange, functional group, and message envelopes similar to those found in ANSI:

- UNB — Header Start Interchange
- UNZ — Trailer End Interchange
- UNG — Header Start Functional Group
- UNE — Trailer End Functional Group
- UNH — Header Start Message
- UNT — Trailer End Message

The headers identify and specify the applicable interchange, functional group, or message, while the trailers serve as a completeness check on the corresponding envelope by means of total count and reference numbers.

The system of acknowledgments works the same way in ANSI as in EDIFACT. It informs trading partners that a transaction has taken place. In case of disputes between trading partners, the acknowledgment may also support the existence of a transaction.

SPECIFIC EXAMPLE

Payments

An analysis of the current version of the X12 and EDIFACT payment message formats shows similar objectives behind the construction of payment-related information. The visible difference between these two formats is the X12 treatment of aggregate information in one transaction set and the EDIFACT segmentation of the same information into several messages. The same types of payment information can be captured, if so desired, in either approach.

The following is a high-level comparison of the two formats for payments:

ASC X12 Version 3020

820	Payment Order/ remittance advice

EDIFACT Status 91.2

PAYORD	Payment order only
PAYTEXT	Payment order and remittance advice
DEBADV	Debit advice
CREADV	Credit advice
CREEXT	Credit and remittance information
REMADV	Remittance advice only

Control Considerations and a General Audit Program for EDI

This appendix provides examples of controls that are appropriate in an EDI environment. The controls are discussed according to financial statement and computer objectives. This appendix also provides a general program for auditing EDI in an integrated environment assuming the use of a VAN, including an illustrative work plan for testing controls over accuracy and completeness of inbound and outbound transactions. These sample audit procedures could be used to obtain evidence that control policies or procedures over EDI are operating effectively, thus enabling the auditor to assess control risk below maximum. It should be emphasized that the procedures are not meant to be prescriptive; the auditor should use professional judgment to decide what procedures should be used in particular circumstances.

Section of Program	Page

UNDERSTANDING THE BUSINESS

This section identifies activities that an auditor should consider as the initial steps in the EDI section of an audit program.

Sample Audit Procedures — Obtain a General Overview of the EDI Function

- Ascertain whether adequate segregation of duties exists for significant areas, including —
  - Authentication with access control and nonrepudiation.
  - Database administration.
  - Certification/accreditation.
  - EDI users and the EDI security administrator.
- Document the internal system flow to determine which fields/processing phases/files are essential and how such items could be tested.
- Review the interconnect administration and procedures of data flow between VANs and trading partners for apparent deficiencies in internal control.

ACCURACY AND COMPLETENESS OBJECTIVES

Receipt of Inbound Transactions

All inbound EDI transactions are accurately received (communication phase), translated (translation phase), and passed to an application (application interface phase), and all inbound EDI transactions are processed only once.

Control Considerations

- Edit checks to identify erroneous, unusual, or invalid transactions prior to updating application.
- Perform additional computerized checking (e.g., trading partner profiles) to assess transaction reasonableness, validity, etc.; consider expert system front ends for complex comparisons.
- Log each inbound transaction on receipt.
- Use control totals on receipt of transactions to verify the number and value of transactions to be passed to each application; reconcile totals between applications and with trading partners.
- Segment count totals built into transaction set trailer by the sender.
- Transaction set count totals built into the functional group header by the sender.
- Batch control totals built into the functional group header by the sender.

- Sequential control numbers built into the interchange header by the sender.
- Confirm validity of sender against trading partner details.
- Use control fields within an EDI message at either the transaction, functional group, or interchange level (often within the EDI header, trailer, or control record):
  - Batch or hash totals.
  - Sequentially number or record count totals.
- Use VAN sequential control numbers or reports.
- Assign in-sequence control numbers to all records received.
- Send an acknowledgment transaction to inform the sender of message receipt; the sender should then match this against a file/log of EDI messages sent.
- Log errors and/or rejects in a queue file and return an appropriate advice to the sender.
- Generate exception reports that are followed up on a timely basis.
- Ensure that duplicate transactions are controlled and reviewed.
- Use edit checks (e.g., reasonableness) within EDI software.
- Provide an electronic audit trail for accountability and tracking.
- Ensure that the system will prevent the overriding or bypassing of data editing.
- Ensure EDI has an electronic interface with the payment system.
- Have supervisors review sensitive transactions.
- Arrange for security over temporary files and data transfer to ensure that inbound transactions are not altered or erased between time of transaction receipt and application update.
- Perform reconciliations on a timely basis to prevent erroneous transactions from affecting the business.
- Maintain the number of messages received/sent and validate with the trading partners from time to time.
- Exchange control totals of transactions sent and received between trading partners at predefined intervals.
- In the processing of individual transactions, use control techniques such as check digits on control fields, loop, or repeat counts not exceeded.

Sample Audit Procedures — Inbound Transactions

- Confirm validity of sender against trading partner details (see accompanying sample work plan).
- Review security over temporary files and data transfer (see accompanying sample work plan).
- Review error recovery procedures.
- Examine EDI sequence control process.
- Test batch or hash total processing to ascertain that it is functioning effectively.
- Sample error processing and advice notification.
- Test for duplicate entries, fields, and records.

- Confirm separation of EDI user and security administrator.
- Identify and test any management overrides.
- Evaluate exception report use, items reported, and actual use.
- Identify supervisor approval of transactions and test controls.

Sample Work Plan

1. *To confirm validity of sender against trading partner details:*

Through interviews with systems personnel and purchasing management and systems users, and through reviews of system documentation, as appropriate —
- Determine how sender identifier is validated and where this occurs in the processing sequence.
- Assess whether this validation is adequate to prevent transactions with invalid identifiers from subsequent inappropriate processing.
- Determine how exceptions are reported and resolved and assess the adequacy of these procedures to appropriately dispose of invalid sender identifiers.
- Determine how the system's list of approved vendors and vendor identifiers is maintained and who has authorization to perform maintenance.
- Assess the adequacy of these procedures to ensure that only currently authorized vendors and their valid identifiers are in this list.

Through reviews of the access control listings —
- Identify all individuals who have access privileges to the system file of approved vendors.
- Compare the control listings to the names of authorized personnel identified above.
- Discuss exceptions, if any, with purchasing management.

Conclude on the effectiveness of this control.

2. *To provide security over temporary files and data transfer to ensure that inbound transactions are not altered between time of transaction receipt and application update:*

Through interviews of systems personnel and review of docmentation, as appropriate —
- Identify the data sets holding inbound transactions awaiting application processing.

Through reviews of the access control listings —
- Identify all individuals who have access privileges to these data sets.
- Discuss with appropriate systems and user personnel to determine the need for this access, and why and how often such access occurs.

Conclude on the effectiveness of this control.

Processing of Inbound Transactions

File update processing occurs in a complete and accurate manner.

Control Considerations

- Generate an automated check of control totals to final file output.
- Generate an automated check of inbound file detail to final outbound file output.
- Flag and store rejected and partially processed entries.
- Assign record sequence control numbers to all inbound transmissions.
- Use standardized default options assigned by users.
- Have an error recovery mechanism that includes identification and correction procedures.
- Deliver reports to appropriate areas for reconciliation purposes.
- Reject invalid transactions before corrupting files.

Sample Audit Procedures — Processing of Inbound Transactions

- Verify control total processing.
- Determine incoming files check to final outbound files.
- Review logs for rejected and partially processed entries to ascertain that they are being identified and resolved.
- Determine the process to sequence and control inbound transmissions.

Sending of Outbound Transactions

All outbound-designated EDI transactions are accurately passed from application (application interface phase), translated (translation phase), and sent (communication phase) only once and on a timely basis.

Control Considerations

- Use control fields within an EDI message at either the transaction, functional group, or interchange level (often within the EDI header, trailer, or control record):
  - Batch or hash totals.
  - Sequentially number all outbound transactions, perhaps using unique sequences for each trading partner or record count totals.
- Use VAN sequential control numbers or reports.
- Match acknowledgment transactions (received from the trading partner) to the client's file/log of EDI messages sent.
- Have error recovery procedures at each phase of EDI processing to ensure that transactions are corrected and reintroduced.
- Provide additional computerized checking (e.g., trading partner profiles) to assess reasonableness of transaction values, quantities, etc.

- Use acknowledgments, transfer protocols such as check sums, and message authentication.
- Secure interim files to ensure that outbound transactions are not altered or erased between time of generation and transmission.
- Build batch control totals into the functional group trailer.
- Build transaction sequence numbers into the interchange.
- Perform reconciliations on a timely basis to prevent erroneous transactions from affecting the business.
- Maintain the number of messages received/sent and validate with the trading partners from time to time.
- Maintain an electronic audit trail for accountability and tracking (e.g., by recording event in a control data base).
- Exchange control totals of transactions sent and received between trading partners at predefined intervals.
- In the processing of individual transactions, use edit checks such as check digits on control fields, loop, or repeat counts not exceeded.

Sample Audit Procedures —Outbound Transactions

- Review error recovery procedures.
- Examine EDI sequence control process.
- Test batch or hash total processing to ascertain that it is functioning effectively.
- Sample error processing and advice notification.
- Test for duplicate entries, fields, and records.
- Confirm separation of EDI user and security administrator.
- Identify and test any management overrides.
- Evaluate exception report use, items reported, and actual use.
- Identify supervisor approval of transactions and test controls.

Processing of Outbound Transactions

File update processing occurs in a complete and accurate manner.

Control Considerations

- Generate an automated check of control totals final file output.
- Generate an automated check of outbound file detail to final inbound file output.
- Flag and store rejected and partially processed entries.
- Assign record sequence control numbers for all outbound transmissions.
- Use standardized default options assigned by users.
- Have an error recovery mechanism that includes identification and correction procedures.
- Deliver reports to appropriate areas for reconciliation purposes.
- Reject invalid transactions before corrupting files.

Sample Audit Procedures — Processing of Outbound Transactions

- Verify control total processing.
- Determine outgoing files check to final inbound files.
- Review logs for rejected and partially processed entries to ascertain that they are being identified and resolved.
- Determine the process to sequence and control outbound transmissions.

AUTHORIZATION OBJECTIVES

Inbound Transactions

Only properly authorized inbound transactions are processed. This includes the objective that inbound EDI messages are from a valid trading partner and that EDI messages contain approved transactions for the given trading partner.

Control Considerations

- Use control fields within an EDI message to verify the identity of the sending trading partner:
  - Identification code
  - Password.
- Control setting up and changing of trading partner details.
- Compare transactions to trading partner transaction profiles (e.g., check the quantity ordered against average, median, and minimum/maximum order levels).
- Match trading partner number to the trading file master file prior to transmission.
- Limit the authority of users within the organization to initiate specific EDI transactions.
- Segregate initiation and transmission responsibilities for high-risk transactions.
- Use digital signatures, dual authorization, smart cards, etc.
- Require management sign-off on programmed procedures and subsequent changes.
- Secure programs from all unauthorized changes.
- Ensure that all payment transactions are logged to a separate file, which is reviewed for authorization before transmission.
- Segregate duties within the transaction cycle (e.g., order entry/approval versus evidence of receipt of goods versus approval of payment), particularly where transactions are automatically generated by the system.
- Ensure that the EDI application will prevent specific types of transactions, such as those over a trading partner's specified dollar limit, from processing.
- Use digital signatures to verify identity.

- Ensure VAN verification of sending trading partner (i.e., via an ID code) before accepting messages for the "mailbox."
- Control report distribution.
- Flag and report rejected transactions.
- Notify transaction originator of the rejected transaction.
- Have input transactions generate advices that are returned to the transaction originator.
- Ensure that EDI transaction advices are sent and are properly reviewed.
- Approve maintenance forms prior to input.

Sample Audit Procedures — Inbound Transactions

- Test EDI report distribution.
- Review reject transaction processing.
- Confirm advice notification process.
- Determine that maintenance forms exist; note date of approval.
- Verify that dollar or specific transaction edits perform as expected.
- Review criteria for various levels of acknowledgment and ascertain that they have been agreed to by the trading partners.
- Ascertain that any special editing rules that are important to positive or negative acknowledgment are well documented and are being used.
- Ascertain that the procedures for reporting irregularities and error/exception handling are well documented and followed.

Outbound Transactions

Only properly authorized outbound transactions are processed. This includes the objective that outbound EDI messages are initiated upon authorization, that they contain only preapproved transaction types, and that they are sent to valid trading partners only.

Control Considerations

- Control setting up and changing of trading partner details.
- Compare transactions with trading partner transaction profiles.
- Match trading partner number to the trading file master file prior to transmission.
- Limit the authority of users within the organization to initiate specific EDI transactions.
- Segregate initiation and transmission responsibilities for high-risk transactions.
- Require document management sign-off on such programmed procedures and subsequent changes.
- Secure programs from all unauthorized changes.
- Ensure that all payment transactions are logged to a separate file, which is reviewed for authorization before transmission.
- Segregate duties within the transaction cycle (e.g., order entry/

approval versus evidence of receipt of goods versus approval of payment), particularly where transactions are automatically generated by the system.

- Segregate access to different authorization processes in a transaction cycle (i.e., ordering, receipt, and payment functions).
- Report large (value) or unusual (e.g., large variations in order quantities) transactions for review prior to or after transmission.
- Log outbound transactions in a secure temporary file until authorized and due for transmission.
- Use computer-based matching between transactions at different points in the processing cycle (e.g., purchase order to receipt to payment).
- Use smart cards and/or PINs to identify authorizing organization or person where payment transactions are generated.

Control Considerations — Authentication

- Provide a digital signature or similar method (e.g., message authentication code, public-key encryption) with each transaction.
- Attach authentication to a document using standard document headers.
- Use a strictly controlled table of valid trading partner information (account number, credit limit, key information, etc.).
- Screen trading partners through third-party service provider.
- Use a message authentication code (MAC) to validate these transactions.
- Log, promptly review, and follow up all transactions failing any validation.
- Provide exception reporting and procedures to detect and follow up authentication failures as soon as possible and before transactions are acted upon.
- Use feasibility/comparison checks within applications and possibly expert systems to review transactions and trading partners against valid profiles of trading partners.
- Where encryption techniques are used, establish effective key management procedures including encryption of keys when transmitted; secure storage of keys (consider tamper-proof encryption hardware); and split keys maintained by separate employees.

Sample Audit Procedures — Outbound Transactions

- Test EDI report distribution.
- Review reject transaction processing.
- Confirm advice notification process.
- Determine that maintenance forms exist, note date of approval.
- Verify that dollar or specific transaction edits perform as expected.
- Review criteria for various levels of acknowledgment and ascertain that they have been agreed to by the trading partners (see sample work plan below).

- Ascertain that any special editing rules that are important to positive or negative acknowledgment are well documented and are being used.
- Ascertain that the procedures for reporting irregularities and error/exception handling are well documented and followed.
- Review use of authentication techniques (see sample work plan below).

Sample Work Plan

Consider completeness and accuracy controls over transmission (for example, use of acknowledgments, transfer protocols such as check sums, and message authentication).

Through discussions with systems personnel, purchasing management, and systems users, and through reviews of selected trading partner agreements, as appropriate —

- Determine the extent to which acknowledgments, check sums, and message authentication are used to ensure accuracy and completeness of transmission of outbound transactions.
- Determine what other techniques management relies on for assurance of accuracy and completeness.

Acknowledgments are EDI transactions that are created and sent by the receiver of transactions to acknowledge receipt of a transaction. Depending on the trading partner agreement, they may be used for each individual transaction or only to acknowledge that a transmission has been received. They may be used for all or only specified transaction types.

- Determine what levels of acknowledgment are expected from trading partners and for what types of transactions.
- Determine whether the client verifies all acknowledgments and informs trading partners of exceptions, if any.
- Determine whether such exceptions have been detected in the audit period and how these were resolved.
- Determine what check sums are computed as outbound transactions are built and whether the trading agreements require the receivers to report exceptions.
- Determine whether such exceptions have been reported in the audit period and how these were resolved.
- Obtain copies of exceptions reported by trading partners for a selected month in which exceptions were noted, and note evidence of appropriate review and disposition.

Message authentication typically involves some form of encryption or similar algorithm and a key, which the sender uses to process a portion of the transaction (for example, the amount element) and create a message authentication code (MAC), which is included in the transaction data segment. The key is known only to the sender and receiver. The receiver uses the algorithm and the key to repeat the computation of the MAC and com-

(continued)

pares this with the MAC contained in the transaction. If they are not equal, the data elements (for example, the amount) received are not the same as those sent, and the message must be rejected and reported for resolution.

- Determine the types of transactions (if any) for which message authentication is used and what provisions are in place to maintain the secrecy of the keys required.
- Determine how trading partners report exceptions and how these are resolved by the client.
- Determine whether such exceptions have been reported in the audit period and how these were resolved.
- Obtain copies of exception reports for a selected month in which exceptions were noted and note evidence of appropriate review and disposition.

Conclude on the effectiveness of this control.

AUDIT TRAIL AND DATA RETENTION OBJECTIVES

Procedures exist to provide accountability and to ensure that data are available as evidence for the auditor.

Control Considerations for Reporting, Logging, and Audit Trails

- Perform reviews of exception reports for follow-up of unusual or unauthorized transactions before they affect internal operations or decision making.
- Holding transactions highlighted as potential problems in a 'suspense' file.
- Provide timely reporting and follow-up of suspense items.
- Secure temporary files from unauthorized access.
- Provide audit and management trails for reconciliation with trading partner acknowledgments and third-party provider reports.
- Define appropriate information and procedures required to reconcile charges from third parties with transaction history on a timely basis.
- Log all transactions (and acknowledgments) at least in semipermanent media, preferably using a secure or nonupdateable medium, protect transaction logs from alteration to retain a valid audit trail for audit purposes.
- Retain the standard document version (e.g., EDIFACT) as initially received for all transmissions (for legal purposes) as well as the translated version (for internal purposes).
- Maintain transaction trails as required for audit, tax (including sales tax), legal and regulatory, and other purposes; this should include critical transactions and events and changes to trading

partner information and should be sufficient and in an appropriate format and medium.

- Maintain a secure copy of transmitted and received messages in their interchanged image (e.g., X12) for use in the event of disputes.
- Build audit trails with authentication coding in each record to prevent fraudulent manipulation of the audit trail.
- Retain logs for an appropriate period, recorded on a medium that is protected, secure, or write once (e.g., laser WORM disks or logging boxes) or in optical form (paper or microfiche).
- Alternatively, give consideration to transmission of key data to an independent third party for retention in case of disputes.
- Ensure that the communications trail facilitates detection of transmission errors, follow-up queries, and appropriate recovery.

Sample Audit Procedures

- Check that output can be traced to source.
- Review input and date stamping.
- Review report identification controls.
- Review and test procedures for logging, updating, and monitoring.
- Review procedures for transaction trail maintenance.

LOGICAL AND PHYSICAL ACCESS SECURITY OBJECTIVES

The general objective is that access to data files, messages, and programs is secure. As part of this objective —

- *Logical access to all EDI and EDI-related software is restricted.*
- *Physical access to EDI facilities and equipment is restricted.*
- *Key functions of EDI/EDI-related transactions are segregated to protect against fraud or error.*

Control Considerations

- Ensure that an adequate level of security is provided by the operating system and that key operating systems security features are enforced consistently.
- Make regular password changes, particularly for essential applications and key personnel.
- Adopt multilevel password systems to restrict access to master file records systems and applications software, etc.
- Log EDI system activity and log and review all on-line transactions.
- Provide an error-detection mechanism.
- Restrict the number of log-on attempts to a minimum.
- Delete log-on IDs immediately upon termination of employment.

- Log off automatically (terminal timeout) to ensure that terminals are not available for unauthorized use.
- Encrypt the password file.
- Have terminal acknowledgment that provides positive identification.
- Log, review, and monitor procedures for security violations or attempted violations.
- Require a full log-on sequence after recovery from "down" status.
- For particularly sensitive functions (e.g., payment transaction generation, if use of passwords is not considered sufficiently secure), consider using dual personnel IDs, smart cards, and digital signature.
- Ensure that data uploaded from personal computers are subject to the normal edit checking and validation that are applied to other input data and are reconciled to control totals of data generated from the personal computer; use "scripts" or other measures to ensure that only designated applications can be accessed.

Sample Audit Procedures

- Test password storage, display, and update procedures.
- Verify that EDI application allows data encryption.
- Review and identify controls for sensitive transactions.
- Review application user profile.
- Verify authority levels for sensitive EDI transactions.
- Determine that EDI system activities are logged.
- Verify EDI network operator access restrictions.
- Verify VAN security procedures and controls.
- Determine that the EDI application will generate transmission status.
- Review EDI recovery procedures, error detection, and tracing of transmissions.
- Determine the use of a security software package to control logical access security.
- Verify password procedures for disclosing, changing, encrypting, and monitoring.
- Validate the EDI user security administrator's authority to grant and revoke access.
- Review EDI terminal time out and identification procedures.

PHYSICAL AND LOGICAL SECURITY FOR SOFTWARE OBJECTIVE

EDI software, application databases, libraries, translators, and utilities will be physically and logically secure, backed up, and maintained.

Control Considerations

- Use a software security package to maintain logical security.

- Ensure that the software security package does not allow for shared passwords.
- Have the database reside in an environment secured by security software.
- Have access authority assigned strictly on a need-to-know basis.
- Ensure that EDI utilities are authorized to be used for production applications and are protected from unauthorized access.
- Have sufficient audit trails of the changes to identify users and uses of utilities.
- Have EDI translator programs perform message acknowledgment; ensure that any "unable to acknowledge EDI messages" require controlled handling.
- The EDI translator verifies message and identifies trading partner.
- The delivery control of libraries is handled and controlled centrally.
- Production libraries are separate from development libraries.
- Code and/or table deliveries are properly authorized.
- All system changes are properly investigated, tested, and reviewed.

Sample Audit Procedures

- Review EDI software and database security.
- Review database access and administrator activities.
- Identify library controls.
- Check segregation of duties.
- Test EDI library and development and testing controls.
- Review file protection and system change control procedures.
- Review EDI utilities that facilitate application interfaces.
- Determine that EDI utilities are restricted, that they identify the authorized user, and that they are tested.
- Test whether the EDI translator programs perform message acknowledgment and identify trading partners.

OBJECTIVE — BACKUP AND CONTINGENCY PLANNING

EDI backup and contingency procedures exist and are tested.

Control Considerations

- Have adequate backup for all EDI files.
- Have a facility to recover the program and data libraries in the case of failure.
- Include program and data libraries in the contingency plan.
- Ensure that operational support staff is familiar with the recovery procedures.
- Ensure that users are familiar with the contingency procedures.

Sample Audit Procedures

- Review EDI contingency backup plan.
- Identify significant roles, user participation, and testing.
- Verify testing process.

OBJECTIVE — COMMUNICATIONS SECURITY

Objectives

- *Ensure that each message is interchanged with the entity's trading partner without excessive delay and without loss or duplication.*
- *Ensure that messages corrupted during transmission can be detected and corrected or retransmitted.*
- *Ensure that communications media and equipment are secured against unauthorized access.*
- *Ensure that transmission messages are retained for an appropriate length of time in an acceptable medium and format to provide protection in the event of a dispute.*

Control Considerations

Security Controls

- Install physically secure cabling between terminals and computers and between computers and external communications connections to reduce the risk of illicit tapping.
- Protect communications controllers and multiplexers from unauthorized access.
- Apply an appropriate mix of controls using communications protocols and their associated security features and security features inherent in document standards.
- Use a secure network delivery service (e.g., X.400) compliant with the security standards, such as those set out by IS0.

Encryption

Use encryption, particularly for high-risk transactions, that addresses the following considerations (at the industry level):

- Messages to be encrypted
- Segments of messages to be encrypted
- Algorithms to be used for encryption of data
- Effective key management practices to limit the capability for encoding and decoding messages
- Symmetric (e.g., DES) encryption versus asymmetric (e.g., RSA) encryption, depending on requirements

- Encryption tools to ensure authenticity of trading partners (proof of end points)
- Whether encryption will be hardware- or software-based (hardware encryption is recommended)
- When encryption is to be provided — during transmission or translation — and for how long a message needs to remain encrypted
- Use of a secure network is not adequate if applications at each end are faulty; therefore, end-to-end encryption, with data enclosed in secure envelopes, is recommended to provide maximum security over data and reduce reliance on network security

Verification

- Consider use of immediate message receipt notification, immediate reporting, and review of high-value/high-impact transactions or other control procedures for high-risk or high-value messages.
- Determine which messages require acknowledgment and which details are to be confirmed.
- Consider use of the following techniques for automatic acknowledgment of transactions from trading partners:
  - Hash totals and control totals
  - Full content acknowledgment of messages received
  - Basic (functional) acknowledgment
- Provide procedures to ensure prompt identification and follow-up on missing acknowledgments; when messages are not acknowledged by the recipient within a specified time period, action should be taken by the sender.
- Check exchange control totals (of transactions transmitted and received) with trading partners at predetermined intervals to ensure completeness of transmissions.

Operational

- Consider communications protocols used in terms of restart and recoverability to reduce the risk of error and delay.
- Address reliability of chosen network solution and capability of selected protocols to detect and correct errors identified (e.g., use of check sums, cyclical redundancy checks, message authentication, etc.).
- Consider manual backup procedures.
- Provide protection over dial-in modems and other communications devices; dial-back modems should utilize separate dial-out lines that are not connected to the internal PABX (PBX) and extension forwarding should be discouraged.
- Appoint or utilize a communications specialist and provide appropriate training to relevant staff.

THIRD-PARTY NETWORKS AND MAILBOX STORAGE OBJECTIVES

Objectives

- *Ensure that the mailbox facility is secured — both physically and logically.*
- *Ensure that the network software promptly identifies and reports on corrupt, improperly addressed, and unauthorized transmissions and that these are followed up.*
- *Ensure that access to the network and mailbox facility is restricted.*
- *Obtain independent confirmation of security provided by the third party and, in particular, the network and mailbox security.*
- *Ensure that adequate records of transactions interchanged are maintained by the third party for an appropriate period.*
- *Ensure that formal agreements with third parties clearly set out the terms, conditions, and charges for services provided and identify the responsibilities of each party including (in the case of service providers) continuity of service and security of information.*
- *Ensure that third-party providers maintain and provide appropriate information to enable follow-up and checking of the status of interchange messages and the costs of third-party services.*

Control Considerations

Logical and Operational Security — Third-Party Responsibilities

- Validate all users requesting access to the network before permitting any access.
- Follow up authentication failures immediately.
- Log all dial-in access.
- Change all network-related passwords on a regular basis.
- Restrict access to authorized users via hardware or software devices (e.g., by using dial-back modems).
- Secure network mailboxes to prevent unauthorized access.
- Provide formal procedures for controlling third-party employee access to mailboxes, authorizing changes to passwords, and specifying the level or method of access to mailboxes.
- Provide the capability to redirect messages to another site as required (e.g., backup processing site) while maintaining effective security.
- Provide appropriate recovery procedures and a fail-safe provision for network and computer equipment in the event of failure.
- Ensure that computer operating systems used by third-party suppliers have minimum security level, such as B1 (per "Orange" book).

Network User Responsibilities

- Retrieve mailbox store and forward messages on a timely basis; the maximum time delay should be specified in the agreement.
- Consider regularly checking whether trading partner mailboxes have been cleared or using functional acknowledgment for crucial messages.
- Consider encrypting data across networks, given that envelope headers will need to be unencrypted.
- Retain responsibility for administrative functions and do not allow the network provider to change passwords, trading partner setup and maintenance, etc.; the third-party provider should not have access to these administrative functions, which should be controlled by a separate security module.

Third-Party Agreements

- If possible, users should obtain copies of independent security reviews of the third-party network, prior to signing any agreements with third parties.
- Third-party service providers will normally provide their own agreement, which should include —
  - Nature of services to be maintained, such as network and mailbox use.
  - Service levels to be maintained (response times, etc.) and backup and contingency arrangements to be provided.
  - Rights and obligations of all parties, including liability for errors.
  - Network and mailbox security, including requirements for timing of mailbox clearing; provision for management and audit trails.
  - Provision for continuity of supply of service and period during which service is to be provided.
  - Responsibility to provide software to minimize the risk of corruption or loss of data during transmission and when in storage.
  - Independent third-party review (industry security) and access available for auditors.
  - Charges for network access, transaction transmission, and provision for alteration to charges; jurisdiction in the event of a dispute.

Glossary of EDI and Other Selected Terms

ANSI (American National Standards Institute). A U.S. organization that publishes standards in a number of areas, notably computer-related standards and standards covering EDI. The most important publication is the X12 standard, widely used in the United States, that defines standard document formats for a number of industries/applications.

Archiving. Generally done for audit, backup, and security purposes, the process of sorting and arranging historic records, usually to maximize the space available in computer systems for current data.

Asymmetric Encryption (Public Key Encryption). A cipher technique whereby different cryptographic keys are used to encrypt ("scramble") a message.

Audit Trail. A chronological record of systems activities that shows all additions, deletions, and changes to both data and software. It enables the reconstruction, review, and examination of a transaction from its inception to output and final results.

Authentication. The process of ensuring that someone who has logged on to a service is a bona fide user of that particular service and is, in fact, the person the user purports to be logging on as. It is also used to validate messages transmitted from one computer service to another.

B1. A security assessment of operating systems specified in the U.S. Department of Defense document known as the "Orange" book, related to how easily an operating system can be penetrated. Scaled from A1 to D2, where A1 is not penetrable.

Backup. A copy of all data and software stored in machine-readable form, for use if the main copies are lost/damaged.

Call Back. The EDI server system that verifies the validity of a dial-up user to ensure that the caller is an authorized user. The process often uses a password-activated call-back modem. The incoming line will be disconnected and the preset number for that user will be called back to set up data communication.

Concurrent Audit Tool. See embedded audit module. Main difference is that it is designed and controlled by the auditor and is linked to (rather than being part of) the client's computer system.

Confirmation. A notification by the mailbox system, or EDI server, by a message or code, that a message sent to a trading partner's mailbox has successfully reached its intended mailbox or has been retrieved by the addressee.

Connectivity. The ability of a particular computer or network architecture to be connected to and integrated with incompatible systems. OSI and X.400 standards address connectivity.

Contingency Plan. A plan to minimize disruption to a business and possible financial loss as a result of loss of or disruption to computer processing.

Corruption. The loss or scrambling of data in a computer storage medium.

DEA (Data Encryption Algorithm). The algorithm that forms part of the Data Encryption Standard (DES).

Data Communications. The transfer of data between distant computer processing sites/devices using telephone lines, microwave, and/or satellite links.

Data Encryption Standard (DES). A symmetric algorithm published as a standard by the U.S. National Institute for Standards and Technology in 1977 to encrypt and decrypt data. It uses a 56-bit key. Eight parity bits may be added to the 56 bits to form a 64-bit value for transmission.

Data Transfer. The physical process of initiating and sending data to a corresponding computer system.

Dial Back. See Call Back.

Dial Up. The act of accessing a network by dialing an access phone number or by initiating a computer to dial the number.

Digital Signature. A technique or procedure by which the sender of a message attaches additional data to the message to form a unique and unforgeable sender identifier. This may, in turn, be checked by the receiver of the message to verify the message's authenticity. The technique uses a form of encryption technology called *public key cryptography*. (The sender and receiver may need additional techniques to identify themselves to each other.)

Direct Transmission (Transfer). Direct transmission of data from one host computer system to another (host to host); host-to-host transmission utilizes a public network or an intermediary means (for example, a mailbox).

Document. Electronic image of a form, such as an invoice or purchase order, that trading partners have agreed to exchange.

Document Standard. A standard format for documents that is agreed to by trading partners, usually in specific industries (e.g., automakers), or that may be designed to apply universally (for example, EDIFACT and ANSI X12).

Document Translation. EDI software translates incoming documents using agreed-upon logic for computer storage. It translates documents into the format in which the receiving party wishes to receive them.

EDI (Electronic Data Interchange). The transfer of structured data, by agreed-upon message standards, from one computer system to another by electronic means.

EDIFACT (Electronic Document Interchange for Administration, Commerce and Transport). The ISO standards that will determine a unified international EDI standard.

EFT (Electronic Funds Transfer). The generic term for sending payment instructions over a computer network.

Electronic Document. See Document.

Electronic Envelope. The technique used to send EDI messages. It involves placing a "header" in front of the message and a "trailer" at the end to enable recognition and authentication.

Electronic Mail. Interpersonal messaging. An individual using a terminal, a PC, or an application can access a network to send an unstructured message to another individual or group of people.

Electronic Trading. A full implementation of EDI, particularly the buying and selling process within an industry or common interest group.

Embedded Audit Module. Programs written and compiled within an application program that perform audit procedures concurrently with application processing.

Encryption. A technique for protecting information within a computer system, on magnetic media and during data transmission. An algorithm transforms the data to render it unintelligible. The process can be reversed to regenerate the original data for further processing.

Firewall. An electronic device that, by not permitting network traffic to pass through it, separates or isolates a network segment from the main network. It does, however, maintain a connection between networks.

Functional Acknowledgment. An automatic response by the EDI server that a message, or batch of messages, has been received intact at the intended mailbox.

Functional Definition. The precise purpose of the message (for example, invoice, purchase order). A specific, but nonexclusive term used in standards-setting.

Functional Group. The identification of one or more messages of the same type; headed by a functional group header service segment and ending with a functional group trailer service segment.

Functional Group Header. The service segment that heads and identifies the functional group.

Functional Group Identifier. The identification of the type of message in the functional group.

Functional Group Trailer. The service segment that ends the functional group.

Gateway. A point of interconnection between one electronic network and another.

Header Area. The portion of the message that precedes the actual body and trailer of the business transaction and that contains information relating to the entire message.

Identifiers (IDs). A unique representation that identifies individual users as they log on to a computer system (or network).

Integrated Test Facility (ITF). "Dummy" entity, such as a fictitious organization, established on a live data file.

Interconnect. The process of linking up two or more third-party networks. It usually involves mailboxes for message delivery between third-party service providers.

JIT (Just in Time). A process adopted by many manufacturers whereby stock is delivered a very short time prior to its being required for use in production. To be effective and reduce inventory holding costs, it requires an effective computerized production scheduling and recording system, as well as a sufficiently advanced industrial infrastructure.

Key Management. The administration and change procedures for the keys used in cryptographic algorithms. It covers methods of generating, distributing, and storing keys.

Leased Line (Dedicated Line). A line permanently assigned to connect two points, as opposed to a dial-up line, which is available and open only when a connection is made by dialing the target machine or network.

Local Area Network. An interconnected group of computers, usually within small geographic bounds.

Log. The act of centrally recording transactions by the systems management function of an EDI service.

Log on (Log in). Connecting to the EDI service by dialing the access number, entering the user ID and password, and then being authenticated as a valid user of the system by the EDI server.

MAC (Message Authentication Code). A generated code resulting from the processing of a data string and a secret key through an appropriate authentication algorithm (for example, DES). It verifies that the data have not been changed.

Mailbox. A repository for messages in an electronic mail system or EDI server. Only authorized messages are allowed into mailboxes. The EDI server authenticates each message before depositing it in the appropriate "pigeon hole" of a mailbox.

Maintenance Procedure. The authorized process mechanism for requests for changes or additions to EDI messages, data segments, or data elements and related procedures.

Message. An identified and structured set of data elements and segments covering the requirements for a specified transaction.

Message Code. A unique reference identifying a message type.

Message Directory. A directory of standard messages. All standards use both these and data dictionaries.

Message Header Segment. The service segment starting and uniquely identifying a message.

Message Standard. The sequence, attributes, and usage of data elements within a message. Used in all document standards (SWIFT, Sll A, etc.).

Message Switching. The circuit routing and direct transfer of a message from one computer to another without any time delay service (for example, a mailbox) or adding of value.

Message Trailer Segment. The service segment ending and uniquely identifying the end of a message.

Modem. An acronym for modulator/demodulator; a device for interfacing communications equipment (for example, terminals, microcomputer nodes) within communication networks.

Network. An interconnected group of computers (including microcomputers) or terminals linked by a transmission facility.

Operating System. A collection of programs that control a computer's internal functions. VAX VMS, MVS XA, MS/DOS, MacIntosh, and UNIX are examples of operating systems.

Packet. A stream of data split up into uniform lengths with checking applied to ensure the completeness, accuracy, and order of the original message.

Packet Network. An electronic message-carrying system that allows one- and two-way communication between computers and terminals in different locations. Packet networks allow different kinds of computers to communicate with one another.

Paperless Trading. The process of exchanging trading documents electronically.

Parity. An error-checking technique used in programming and data communication to ensure receipt of complete and valid data.

Passwords. A protected string of characters or words that authenticates a computer user, a specific response, or an access type.

Polling. A method of controlling transmission of data by inquiring of each particular computer or terminal (in sequence) in a network if it has data to transmit.

Protocol. A set of codes that controls the transmission and receipt of data sent between various communication devices.

Public Key Cryptography. See Asymmetric Encryption.

Public Key Encryption. See Asymmetric Encryption.

Qualified Data Element. A data element whose precise meaning is conveyed by an associated qualifier.

Qualifier. An element of data that gives a qualified data element or segment a specific meaning.

Queue. A group of items (for example, jobs, packets, etc.) waiting for service by a processor.

Receive (Receiving Computer). A (temporarily) passive computer in an EDI network. The computer receives or retrieves EDI documents, directly or via a mailbox.

Record. A collection of related items of data treated as a unit. Fields are the items contained therein.

Script. A program that logs a user directly into an application (or a specific menu option within an application).

Section Control Segment. A service segment used to separate header, detail, and summary sections of a message where necessary to avoid ambiguities in the message segment content.

Security. A generic term generally describing the method adopted to protect data from loss, corruption, unauthorized access, and retrieval.

Segment. A predefined and identified set of normally functionally related data elements identified by the sequential positions within the set. A segment starts with a segment tag and ends with a segment terminator. It can be a service or a user data segment.

Segment Code. A code that uniquely identifies each segment as specified in a segment directory.

Segment Name. One or more words identifying a data segment concept.

Segment Specifications. The contents, structure, and attributes of a segment.

Segment Tag. A unique identifier of a segment.

Segment Terminator. A syntax character that is used to identify the end of a segment.

Send. To transmit data.

Server. The computer at the heart of an EDI system.

Service Segment. A segment required to service the interchange of user data.

Store and Forward. The term commonly applied to a messaging (for example, electronic mail) system in which a message is stored before it can be delivered to a third party. The term implies that the mailbox system itself performs delivery to the addressee, that is, direct delivery.

Store and Retrieve. The situation whereby a message is sent to a mailbox and resides there until retrieved by the addressee accessing the addressee's own mailbox, or possibly, purged to an archive file if it lies dormant for a predetermined period of time.

Summary Area. The portion of the message that follows the body and that contains summary information relating to the entire message.

Symmetric Encryption. The situation whereby two trading partners share one or more secret keys. No one else can read their messages. A different key (or set of keys) is needed for each pair of trading partners.

Systems Administration. The function of allocating mailbox addresses, user IDs, and passwords and of checking security routines, bulk printing, audit routines, housekeeping, statistics, and billing.

Systems Management. The tasks involved in keeping a network in service by providing access to valid users. It also involves security, logging, provision of statistics, billing, and central services such as printing.

Telecommunication. Communication between computers or peripheral devices in different locations. It often takes place over long distances and is usually carried out via telephone lines, radio waves, or a satellite-transmission apparatus.

Third Party. A party, such as a VAN, involved in the trading relationship with whom the company is not directly trading.

Time Out. The situation whereby a time limit is established for a certain action, for example, receipt of a message; when the set time is exceeded, the message is rejected and the end user is so informed.

Trading Partner. An organization with which a company establishes a trading relationship.

Trading Partner Agreement. A contract between two EDI trading partners. It generally addresses, for example, EDI communications, trade terms, and conditions relating to merchandise returns and warranties.

Transaction. A single completed transmission, for example, the transmission of a single invoice over an EDI network.

Transaction Set. The name given to a complete trading document, for example, an invoice, sent electronically.

Transcription Error. A mistake or omission in the copying of information from one document to another, whether done clerically or via a keyboard.

User ID. A password and identifier that enables an end user to sign on to a computer system.

User Manual. A document that sets out procedures agreed upon by two trading parties, including security arrangements, recovery procedures, and follow-up of unusual transactions.

Validation. The process of checking whether a document is of the correct type for a particular EDI system and whether it comes from or is going to an authorized user. This includes all of the editing and syntax checking involved in standards conformance.

VAN (Value-Added Network). A third party that provides network and store and forward (mailbox) services.

WORM Disk. A Write-Once Read-Many disk enables "read only" access to all users. Data cannot be updated or deleted (unless the complete disk is overwritten).

Selected Bibliography

Ansary, H.J. "The Significance of EDI to Corporate Survival in the 1990s," *The Journal of Electronic Data Interchange* (Volume 6, Number 1, 1993), pp. 10–13.

Baldwin, T., and B. Williams. "IT and the Auditor: The Next 10 Years," *Accountancy* (October 1990).

Bodnar, G.H. "Nonrepudiation of Paperless Workpapers," *Internal Auditing* (Fall 1991) pp. 77–81.

Burke, D.P. "Gearing up for EDI," *Financial Executive* (May/June 1993), pp. 25–29.

Canadian Institute of Chartered Accountants (CICA). *EDI for Managers and Auditors,* 2d ed. (Toronto, CICA, 1993).

Chalmers, L.S. "Data Security and Control — New Technology Introduces New Risks," *Journal of Accounting and EDP* (Winter 1990), pp. 28–30.

Chan, S. "Managing and Auditing EDI Systems Development," *CMA Magazine* (November 1991), pp. 12–15.

Coleman, A. "EDI: An Application Often Without a Responsible Owner," *IS Audit & Control Journal* (Volume II, 1994), pp. 14–16.

Denroche, J. "EDI and the Collection of Federal Government Revenue," *Canadian Treasurer* (October/November 1991), pp. 19–22.

Doty, Jr. E.A., and D.R. Hines. "Internal Controls for Financial EDI," *Financial & Accounting Systems* (Winter 1992), pp. 27–31.

EDI Council of Australia and the EDP Auditors Association. *EDI Control Guide* (Sydney, Australia: EDICA, 1990).

EDP Auditor's Foundation, Inc. *EDI: An Audit Approach,* Monograph Series 7 (New South Wales, Australia: EDP Auditor's Foundation, Inc., April 1994).

Financial Executives Research Foundation (FERF). *Electronic Data Interchange and Corporate Trade Payments* (Morristown, NJ: FERF, 1988).

Galloway, D. "Auditors Join the EDI Underground," *CA Magazine* (October 1989), pp. 64–66.

Goldfarb, M.G. "A Password to Computer Security," *Financial Executive* (July/August 1992), pp. 34–36.

Gunther, L.J. "Implementing EDI in a Controlled Environment," *IS Audit & Control Journal* (Volume II, 1994), pp. 42–46.

Hamdi, B.J. "Electronic Authorization and Authentication," *CGA Magazine* (April 1994), pp. 44–47, 72.

Hansen, J., and N. Hill. "Control and Audit of Electronic Data Interchange," *MIS Quarterly* (December 1989), pp. 403–413.

Holley, C.L. and S.S. Fitzgerald. "Auditing Electronic Funds Transfer Systems," *The Internal Auditor* (June 1982), pp. 16–20.

Institute of Internal Auditors Research Foundation. *Audit, Control, and Security of Paperless Systems,* based on the proceedings of the 1990 Advanced Technology Forum.

Institute of Internal Auditors Research Foundation. *Systems Auditability and Control (SAC)* (Altamonte Springs, Fla: Institute of Internal Auditors Research Foundation, 1991).

Jarrett, C.V. "The Future Mission of Audit," *The Magazine of Bank Administration* (August 1983), pp. 22–28.

Jenkins, G., and R. Lancashire. *The EDI Implementation Handbook* (Toronto, Ont.: Electronic Data Interchange Council of Canada, 1992).

Jones, P. *Essentials of EDI Law* (London, ON: Electronic Data Interchange Council of Canada, 1992).

Lauzon, Y., and C. Botting. "Just the Facts: 1992 Survey of EDI in Canada," *The Journal of Electronic Data Interchange* (Volume 6, Number 1, 1993) pp. 18–23.

McCusker, T. "EDI II to the Rescue," *Datamation* (May 15, 1992), pp. 60–64.

Meier, J.J. "EDI — A Practical Approach," *CMA Magazine* (September 1992), pp. 29–31.

Morris, S. "Electronic Data Interchange — IT Technology or Business Strategy," *Accountancy SA* (August 1993), pp. 4–8.

National Science and Technology Council. "High Performance Computing and Communications: Technology for the National Information Infrastructure" (Supplement to the President's Fiscal Year 1995 Budget) (Washington, DC: Office of Science and Technology Policy, 1994.)

Reimel, J.C. "Audit Implications of EDI," *AICPA InfoTech Update* (Fall 1992), pp. 1–4.

Sadhwani, A.T., I.W. Kim, and J. Helmerci. "The Impact of Electronic Data Interchange on Internal Controls," *Journal of Accounting and EDP* (Fall 1989), pp. 23–31.

Seveny, G.M. "EDI — An Emerged Technology," presented at the *Canadian Conference on Auditing & Computer Technology* (March 1992).

Slesinger, G. "Electronic Data Interchange: How to Make It Work," *Journal of Corporate Accounting and Finance* (Autumn 1992), pp. 3–10.

Society of Management Accountants of Canada (SMAC). Exposure Draft, "Implementing Electronic Data Interchange" (Hamilton, ON: SMAC, 1992).

Society of Management Accountants of Canada. Management Accounting Issues Paper 2, "The Role of Management Accounting in Electronic Data Interchange" (Hamilton, Ont.: SMAC, October 1993).

Sorkin, H.L. "Nonrepudiation: Bits and Signatures," *Internal Auditing* (Winter 1991), pp. 24–31.

Stelzer, J.L. "What Price Data Security," *EDI Forum* (1992), pp. 78–84.

Takach, G. "Canadian EDI Trading Partner Agreement," *The Journal of Electronic Data Interchange* (Volume 6, Number 1, 1993) pp. 59–62.

Vahtera, P. "Electronic Data Interchange: The Auditor's Slant," *EDPACS* (November 1991), pp. 1–13.

Vézina, G. "The Accountant's Role in EDI," *CMA Magazine* (February 1991), pp. 26–29.

Westover, L., and T. O'Mara. "Security and Control in Financial EDI: The Treasury Manager's Role," *Canadian Treasurer* (August/September 1993), pp. 30–34.

Williams, J. "Beware the March of EDI — Implications of Electronic Data Interchange for Accountants and Auditors," *Accountant's Journal* (December 1990), pp. 20–26.

Wise, T.M. "EDI: Progressing Toward the Paperless Office," *Internal Auditing* (Summer 1989), pp. 75–81.

Wright, B. "Controlling EDI," *Management Accounting* (August 1991), pp. 46–49.

Wright, M. "Accounting in a Paperless Office," *Australian Accountant* (August 1990), pp. 45–48.

Yu, J.W. "The Paperless EDI Environment," *CGA Magazine* (September 1993), pp. 40–42.

Zoladz, C. "Auditing in an Integrated EDI Environment," *IS Audit & Control Journal* (Volume II, 1994), pp. 36–40.